Child-
proofing
Your
Marriage

Child-proofing Your Marriage

KEEPING YOUR MARRIAGE A PRIORITY
DURING THE PARENTING YEARS

DR. DEBBIE L. CHERRY

LIFE JOURNEY®

Bringing Home the Message for Life

An Imprint of Cook Communications Ministries
COLORADO SPRINGS, COLORADO • PARIS, ONTARIO
KINGSWAY COMMUNICATIONS, LTD., EASTBOURNE, ENGLAND

Life Journey® is an imprint of
Cook Communications Ministries, Colorado Springs, CO 80918
Cook Communications, Paris, Ontario
Kingsway Communications, Eastbourne, England

CHILDPROOFING YOUR MARRIAGE
© 2004 by Debbie L. Cherry, Ph.D.

Published in association with Yates & Yates, LLP, Attorneys and Counselors, Orange, California.

First printing 2004
Printed in the United States of America
1 2 3 4 5 6 7 8 9 10 Printing/Year 08 07 06 05 04

Editor: Susan Martins Miller
Cover Design: Two Moore Designs/Ray Moore
Cover Photo: © Royalty Free/Corbis

Library of Congress Cataloging-in-Publication Data applied for
ISBN: 0781441447

To Taffeta, Tiara, and Talon,

My three beautiful children who have served
to teach this parenting team the importance
of staying strong and staying together,

Thank you, and
I love you the "mostest"!

CONTENTS

ACKNOWLEDGMENTS

I thank God, first and foremost, for every blessing He has given, every lesson He has taught, and every opportunity He has presented for me to share His love!

In addition to Him, there are so many people I would like to thank and acknowledge. Each of these people has played a special role in my life and has helped bring the concepts in this book to life. I say "thank you" to …

My amazing husband, Jim, and our three children—for sacrificing so much during this very difficult and hectic past year. You each showed me love and patience in your own unique way, and it was that love that helped me get through the many long hours, days, and weekends of writing.

The whole team at Cook Communications—for taking a chance on book number two. Thank you for believing in me and my message, and for making me look better than I ever could without you.

Terry Whalin—for seeing something in me and encouraging me to get it out! You have been my champion in such a way that I'm afraid no one will ever be able to duplicate. Thanks for spoiling me!

Dr. Kathy Wingo—for sharing with me many of the pearls you have gained through your years of counseling and life experience. This book wouldn't be the same without them.

Gary Smalley—for your never-ending support, encouragement, guidance, and wisdom. I wouldn't be where I am without you.

Dr. Gary Chapman—for lending your words, support, and name to this book. I am blessed beyond words.

The team at Yates & Yates—and especially Chris Ferebee—for putting up with me and my strong personality. Thank you for your wise counsel every step of the way.

And, finally, to all those couples who have shared their own personal stories and struggles with me. May God bless each of you with a "childproofed" marriage that keeps on growing and growing and growing.

FOREWORD

For over thirty years, I have been sitting in the counseling office listening to couples pour out their pain. For me, nothing has been sadder than those couples who have focused on parenting their children while neglecting their marriages. They were deluded into thinking that the best thing they could do was to seek to meet the children's needs. Yet, they failed to recognize that when they didn't meet each other's needs, they were setting the worst of examples for their children.

My wife and I learned early on that we had to focus on each other if we were to become good parents. We had serious struggles in the early years of our marriage, before the children came. When they arrived, we knew that we could not let those little treasures weasel their way between us. We loved the children devotedly, but more than anything, we wanted to have the kind of marriage that would serve as an example for them. I remember how hard we worked to get the children to bed early so we could have time together. Karolyn chose to be a "stay-at-home mom," and we agreed to live on less so we could have time for marriage and parenting. I'm not suggesting it was easy. I am saying that we have no regrets. The children are now gone, and we are still together—loving, learning, and growing.

I am convinced that one of the best things any of us can do for our children is to provide them with a strong marital model. Children need to know that their parents love not only them, but each other. The child's sense of security grows as he/she sees parents loving each other. To put your marriage on hold for eighteen or more years while you raise the children is not only detrimental to the marriage, it is devastating to the children.

We must learn to "childproof" our marriages during those parenting years, or we will soon learn that the marriage withers and dies. When the parental team breaks down and begins to disintegrate, the children become the biggest losers. They lose their family unit, which is where they build their sense of security. When children don't feel secure, their whole world seems to unravel. No amount of baseball, dance, piano lessons, or toys can make up for that kind of loss.

As a matter of fact, recent research has shown that when the family unit falls apart, so do the kids. Children from broken homes show a higher rate of

> Academic problems
> Dropping out of school
> Promiscuity
> Teen pregnancy
> Alcohol and drug use/abuse
> Running away
> Emotional and behavioral problems
> Violence
> Delinquency
> Suicide
> Poverty as an adult

And that's just to name a few. So, if you are thinking that you are doing the best for your child when you put your spouse on the back burner and your kids as number one, you are sorely mistaken. Although children obviously require our time and attention (and our money, too), they do not require *all* of our time or attention (or money). If we hope to influence the next generation, we must experience a change of focus. Of course we are interested in protecting our children from all those things I just listed, and the best way to do that is to help marriages stay together. And that is the focus of this wonderful book that you hold in your hand.

I wish Karolyn and I would have had a book like *Childproofing*

Your Marriage to help us with practical ideas on building a strong marriage while we were raising our kids. We had to learn things the hard way, but you have a chance today, through the help of this book, to learn how to keep your marriage as your top priority so you will be able to grow older and happier and stronger together. In this book, Debbie has done a wonderful job of presenting the major challenges that we as parents face during all the different stages of parenting. She has a fresh and engaging way of sharing challenges from her own marriage/parenting experiences that will keep you turning the pages and challenging yourself to start making changes today.

Join us in our goal of helping marriages grow stronger—even while raising children—and in stopping marriages from falling apart. As we succeed in doing that, we will be succeeding in strengthening our family units and therefore providing the very best for our children. While it may not be easy to continue focusing on and building your marriage while raising your children, it is essential to the long-term health of both. So if you can't seem to do it for yourselves ... do it for your kids! If you truly want to be the best parents you can be ... work to become the best couple you can be.

May God bless you and yours,
GARY D. CHAPMAN, PH.D.

THE GAME OF THE CENTURY

Chuck: Good afternoon, folks! Welcome to the Pregame Show. I'm Chuck Itall and I'm glad you joined us. For the next half hour, we will be giving you the inside scoop on the two teams taking the field today to battle it out in "The Game of the Century"—the Parents and the Kids. As most of you know, we have been following this game for years. In the past few decades, we definitely have seen a trend of field dominance by the Kids team. The same is proving true so far this season as well. Coming into today's game, the Kids are our audience's 2:1 favorite. The determining factor of who will win lies in the preparation of the Parents team.

The only way this underdog Parents team can pull out a win today is if their practice schedule over the past several weeks pays off. Have they finally pulled together and learned to communicate? We can only hope. However, earlier in the season, the Parents team suffered from major internal turmoil. Fights on the sidelines and in the locker rooms were the norm, and everyone knew they weren't coming onto the field unified. The teams they have faced all season have eaten them alive through a "divide and conquer" defense plan. And that is what this Kids team is planning to continue. Although the Kids are still considered the favorite over the Parents team today, rumor has it that this Parents team has pulled it together. You may want to listen carefully before placing your final bets, because there may be some surprises ahead.

To start off our Pregame Show with a bang, let's turn it over to Genie Ology, our resident historian on "The Game of the

Century," for some highlights of the trends of dominance in the past. Genie ...

Genie: Thank you, Chuck. The rivalry between these two teams goes back as far as time. The battles have been harsh at times, but as we've watched over the years, the Parents have almost always come out on top. Their team has a reputation for being tough and strict, and their authority has dominated the playing field. That is, until just a few short decades ago. That's when we started to see a real shift in the power. Actually, as these two teams have met recently, it has proven to be total disaster for all involved. Let me explain.

It seemed that the Kids were developing some new skills and becoming a real challenge for the Parents. They began to dominate the field with their stubborn independence, rebellious maneuvers, and "below-the-belt" tactics. They fine-tuned their ability to divide and conquer the opposing team and developed secret strategies to sabotage their opponent's practice schedule and workout time. Over the past several years, these techniques have rendered more than one Parents team helpless on the field. The Parents have been showing up on game day unprepared, out of shape, exhausted, and unorganized. They either do not have a playbook or they are not playing out of the same book. Within the team, various members are calling different plays, resulting in total chaos on the field. This makes the Kids' job that much easier.

Over these past few decades, as we have watched the Kids team dominate the field, we have noticed a huge increase in the internal fighting of the Parents team. This quickly leads to the Parents unraveling, which signals the beginning of the end of the game. They come onto the field in turmoil, and things only get worse from there. As a matter of fact, on more than one occasion, some members of the Parents team appeared to switch sides in the middle of the game. It's as if they were more on the Kids team than the Parents team, and they begin to sabotage the efforts of the rest of the Parents team. We have seen Parents team members actually telling the Kids the plays from the Parents' playbook and refusing to support their own team during the game. Before long, the Parents team self-destructs and ends up walking off the field in opposite directions.

An interesting note here is that as the Parents terminate their union, the Kids team also begins to unravel. Without a formidable opponent that can provide structure and rules for the game, they realize they do not understand the game anymore. They admit that they had been mimicking the plays of the Parents team—now there's nothing to mimic. They flounder and can't finish the game on their own. They are not celebrating a victory, because they realize there is no game without the other team. If there is no game, there are no winners.

Chuck, we can only hope that something changes. Maybe this is the year that the game gets played through to the end. Back to you.

Chuck: Yes, indeed, we do hope this is the year for change. Thank you, Genie, for that report. And as I mentioned earlier, there are rumors of major changes on the horizon. Under new management, the Parents team has worked all season to overcome the things that have brought devastation in the past, and they are ready to play with a new set of guidelines. In an interview earlier today, we asked the Parents what they were doing differently to help them remain unified till the end of the game. Here are some excerpts from that interview.

Reporter: Is it true that you have placed your team under some new management?

Parent 1: Well, actually it's more like going back to our original manager—God. You see, God is the one who developed this concept. As a team, we used to be much better at following His guidance and suggestions about how to best play this game. But then a while back, we decided to fire Him and thought we could figure this whole thing out ourselves. Well, it's no secret how well we've done. As a matter of fact, it's all over the papers how we've failed miserably and how our failures as a team have affected the Kids team as well.

We finally realized we needed the originator of the game back on board if we were to have any hope of pulling this thing off. When we approached Him and asked if He would return as our manager, He was more than willing. And here we are, in better shape coming into the game than we have been in years. We know it will still be a battle, but we expect to be able to stay committed to seeing it through all the way to the end because we have in place several essential elements to staying in the game.

Reporter: So what exactly are some of these "essential elements"?

Parent 2: Well, for starters, we have learned that the team is only as healthy as each of its individual members. In other words, we have had to do quite a bit of personal training. We have focused on getting physically, emotionally, and spiritually healthy. We have pushed ourselves beyond what we thought were our personal limitations, which we had based on our past experiences. We now know how we can learn from our past without having to repeat it, which was very good news—we really are tired of losing.

Reporter: So you're telling me that each of you getting healthier personally is going to keep you from walking off the field in the middle of the game?

Parent 1: Well, not that alone, but in part, yes. As we become healthier, we have more to contribute to the team. Another essential element we have worked on all season is valuing each other. As you know from watching us just last season, we have been a very selfish team—now that's an oxymoron if I've ever heard one. Many of the fights among ourselves that you and the fans have watched were about "who's number one." We all just wanted to be on top, to call the plays, to get our own way. And guess where that got us? Yep, nowhere. We all wanted to win so badly—and were sure that our way was the only or the best way to win—that we fought each other and pretty much did the other team's job for them. It really has been a mess.

But that's all about to change. As you watch us on the field today, you are going to see a brand-new concept of focusing on the other's needs more than on what we want. We have the same goal now—to complete the game as winners, and we know how to work together to meet that goal. We have learned the concept of teamwork.

Reporter: I can hardly wait to see this. If what you are saying is true, it will be a whole new game out there today. What about the many different playbooks your team has used in the past? It was almost humorous a couple of seasons ago when the press was scanning the sidelines between plays and your team was seen fighting over which of several different playbooks you were going to use. How is that going to be different today?

Parent 3: Thank you so much for reminding us of that horrible moment in history. Well, you're right. I guess in hindsight it was humorous to the outside observer. But I remember being in the middle of that fight, and it was anything but humorous at the time. A huge part of the problem was that each of us had our own playbook. There wasn't anything necessarily wrong with any of them. The problem was that none of us had taken time to study anyone else's playbook. We understood only our own plays and were frantically trying to explain them to each other. This is not something you can do in the few seconds you have between plays. This season, we have taken time to study each other's playbooks and have taken the best from each and compiled them into one unified playbook that now governs the Parents team.

Reporter: So if you had to sum up all these changes for us, what would you say?

Parent 2: More than anything else, we have learned to make each other—not the game or our opponent, but each other—number one! We have learned that unless our team is united and committed to each other for the long haul, unless we stay connected throughout the game, we may not finish the game as a team. And that's really what we want more than anything—to remain together as a team for the rest of our lives.

Reporter: That sounds great. Is there anything else that you would like to share with the fans today?

Parent 1: Yes, there's one more important thing to note. We know that we may still lose a few games to the Kids. But we will play our best game, and hopefully it will have a lasting effect on the members of the Kids team. Because, you know, eventually many of them will be drafted onto a Parents team themselves, and we're hoping that they will be successful because of what we are doing here today.

Reporter: That's an excellent concept. Thank you for being here with us today, and I hope all you've learned will prove to benefit the whole game. Now back to you, Chuck.

Chuck: Well, the Parents definitely sound more confident and unified. I guess we will soon see if this makes a difference in the outcome of the game. Shortly after that interview with the Parents team, we thought it would be interesting to see what the Kids thought. So we showed the interview to the Kids, and here is what they had to say.

Reporter: Well, Kids, there you have it. You have just heard your opponents explain what they have learned and how they are approaching this game today. How does that make you feel?

Kid 1: Believe it or not, this is exactly what we've been hoping for. Although we have proven ourselves to be a formidable opponent these past few decades, we know that our ability to play this game falls apart when the opposing team falls apart. We obviously are not capable of playing this game when we are left to our own devices. When we are playing against the Parents, we are constantly watching and learning from them. We refine our skills based on what we see them doing. And unfortunately, when they decide to fight among themselves or completely walk off the field, we end up doing the same. And as you know, for several years now, you and the fans have been greatly disappointed in how the game has been played and have begun to lose hope of seeing the game through to completion.

Kid 2: But based on what the Parents shared in that interview, there may be hope again. Of course, we will still use all of our well-developed skills of sabotage, rebellion, divide and conquer, and trying to steal their time together, because that's what we are good at. But we are actually hoping that the Parents come into this game more unified, in shape, and ready to play. If they are prepared, then our tactics will not result in destroying their team, and we can all make it to the end of the game. After all, that's really all we want— to finish the game. This bailing out midstream or even right at the end is for the birds. If they aren't committed to their own team, then they shouldn't be playing in this game. But if they are ready to stand their ground as a unified, committed team, then we will play, and we will all end up the winners.

Reporter: Out of the mouths of babes. Sounds like this Kids team is not as interested in winning as much as they are in being a part of the game all the way to the end. And that's really what we all are hoping for, isn't it, folks? A clean game that goes all four quarters and then both teams come out winners. Chuck.

Chuck: Okay, I've just been told it's game time, so here we go. And there's the kick off ...

Are You Ready to Play?

If you are reading this book, you are probably about to begin or are smack dab in the middle of your own personal "Game of the Century." When a married couple changes from being just two to being a family, the challenges of keeping a marriage strong and growing increase. And the biggest challenge of all is remembering that you are still a couple. The parenting role can be overwhelming and all-encompassing, and if you are not careful, the marital relationship may get lost in the hustle and bustle of daily life. Not choosing to childproof your marriage could prove detrimental to the union the two of you formed before God. You were married before you had children (hopefully), and if you want to remain married after your children are grown and gone, then you must spend time during the parenting season to protect your marriage and keep it growing.

Throughout part 1 of this book, you will learn about nine essential elements that childproof your marriage. These elements apply to every stage of parenting. Applying them will help you feel connected and strong as a team. Part 2 addresses each of the main stages of parenting and provides encouragement for parents in each stage. You will read about the specific challenges of each stage along with specific ways to nurture your relationship while meeting those particular challenges. I want to encourage and assure each of you that you really can continue to grow closer in your marriage as your children grow up. Regardless of which stage you are in, commit today to making your relationship with each other your priority (second only to your relationship with God), and both you and your children will end up winners.

PART ONE

THE ESSENTIAL ELEMENTS OF MARITAL SURVIVAL

CHAPTER ONE

WHERE DID I COME FROM?

Essential Element 1: Understanding the Family Tree

Take a minute and imagine that you are an athlete who has dreamed your whole life of being a part of a winning team—maybe a team that would win an Olympic medal or a Super Bowl ring. Do you think you could just show up for tryouts one day—having never even trained for the sport—and get accepted onto the team, no questions asked? I don't think so.

A more realistic view would involve training for the big leagues from as soon as you could toddle across the floor. By the time the tryout day arrived, you would have clocked years of practice and learning time. You would know your sport and your position. You would be aware of what you expected from your team and what they expected from you. You would not only have been working to improve your strengths, but to identify your weak areas. You would have evaluated the coaching you had received compared to other players in the sport and would already be in the process of overcoming any bad habits you might have developed.

It is not likely that you would make the team if you could not even answer the basic question of who had been coaching you through the years and demonstrate what you had learned. People making the team selections would want to know that you are aware of your strengths and weaknesses, and what you are doing to improve on both.

None of us would expect an athlete to become a member of a winning professional team without being able to do what I have just described. However, isn't that a little like what each of us has done? Those of us who are married, anyway. We showed up on selection day for a much more important team—the marriage team—without having spent much, if any, time considering our past coaching or training. How many of us really took time to consider our training for this team? In reality, we have all spent our entire lives training to become a husband or wife and parent. But have you taken time to evaluate the kind of training you received? Can you adequately describe your coaches and the impact they have had on your views of this game called marriage? Can you identify what they taught you—both good and bad? Do you know what parts of your training you want to continue and what parts need to be replaced with healthier habits?

Understanding where you have come from and who and what have formed your thoughts and beliefs about both marriage and parenting is the first essential element of marital survival. This chapter will focus on helping each spouse identify what he or she learned about marriage and parenting from the family of origin. None of us had perfect parents, but we can and do learn from whatever example was set before us. As you realistically evaluate your own childhood, you can pick and choose which elements of marriage and parenting you want to keep and which you want to change. Having a poor example of parents is no excuse for being a poor spouse or parent yourself! You have the choice to change!

Looking in the Rearview Mirror

A highly respected colleague of mine once shared an illustration that I have used many times with people as they consider the impact of the past on the present and future. Near the center of a piece of paper, she drew a rectangular shape that took up less than a quarter of the page. Then she asked me what it was. Having no idea where she was going, I said, "A loosely drawn rectangle?" She chuckled and said, "Well, yes. But actually it's a rearview mirror." She proceeded to describe how she explains this to the people she counsels.

Your past is important, but not "all important." Becoming overly focused on your past would be like trying to drive a car while staring into the rearview mirror. If you are planning to drive in reverse, that might be okay. But I don't know too many people who want their lives going backward. If you are like most of us and hope that you are moving forward and making progress in your life, then focusing on the rearview mirror could be devastating.

Let's consider the other extreme—driving while ignoring the rearview mirror. How well do you think that would work? It might not be bad for awhile, as long as you were only going straight. No lane switches, turns, or quick stops. I actually had a chance to try this. One day, the rearview mirror in my van fell off, and it was a few days before my husband, Jim, had a chance to put it back on. So for about three days, I got to experience driving without access to what was going on behind me. (Yes, I know there are side mirrors, but I rarely use them—and besides, that doesn't work for my example.) At times, this didn't really bother me because I was just headed straight down the highway, things were going smoothly, and I was really not concerned with what was going on behind me.

But on one occasion, the importance of the rearview mirror was made very clear.

I was driving along, singing to the radio and minding my own business, when all of a sudden I was jolted out of my own little world by the sound of screeching tires and horns blowing behind me. I looked up into the space where my rearview mirror should have been, only to remember that it was not there. About that time, a little yellow sports car came flying around me at warp speed and scared me half to death. I had had no idea that he was even there. I was finally able to turn around to see behind me, but by then the crisis seemed to be over. I said a quick prayer, thanking God for protecting me from I'm not sure what, but I knew by the racing of my heart that I had been in danger. By the time my heart slowed down and I was able to consider what had happened, the little yellow car was out of sight. And although I was safe (this time), I realized that because I had no glimpse into what was going on behind me I was completely vulnerable to it. I had no idea what danger was approaching and therefore could not make the needed adjustments to keep myself safe. The value of the rearview mirror became real to me that day. That very evening, Jim found the time to put the mirror back on.

The purpose of the rearview mirror is to provide perspective. To be able to drive your car safely down the highways and byways of life with all the twists and turns, it is necessary to be able to check in periodically with where you have been and what may be coming from behind you. Just as driving a car is safer with a rearview mirror, maneuvering your life is also much easier and safer if you have a proper perspective on your past. Just as the rearview mirror takes up only a small part of your visual field when driving, your past should take up only a small part of your vision for your life. Never let your past become so all-encompassing that it blocks your view of what lies ahead. But don't ignore your past to the point that its pain and dangers can sneak up and overtake you. Your past is there to help give you perspective about where you have been, not to control where you are going.

Identifying the Color of Your Glasses

Now that you understand how a proper perspective of your past affects your ability to move forward into your future, it is time to consider evaluating your past. As you do this, it is important to consider what type of "glasses" you are wearing. Each of us sees our world, including our past, through a particular set of lenses. If we are not careful, the type of glasses we put on can distort what we are trying to see.

Rose-colored glasses. These are just about everyone's favorite. We would all love to live in a world that is perfect, and that is what these glasses help us to believe. As we slip these glasses on, everything we see seems to change. A gleaming pink color overlays everything and transforms even slightly ugly memories and events to things of beauty. And it actually seems that some of those most bothersome remembrances just disappear, or at least they aren't obvious to us from behind these lenses.

Wearing rose-colored glasses while attempting to evaluate your past will distort events in a positive way. With these glasses on, some people will even reach the point of believing that their family is perfect and that they had a perfect childhood. Many of us had some wonderful times growing up and had a close and connected family. But I have never met the perfect family. Because we are all humans and we all make mistakes, none of us had the perfect family. As you evaluate your family, it is important to understand this. Identifying the parts of your family of origin that were less than perfect is not being disloyal or disrespectful to your parents. It is simply being real so that you can learn to be real in your current family.

Dark-colored glasses. Although we may say that we do not want to wear these glasses, many of us end up choosing to put them on at least part of the time. Wearing dark glasses as you look into and evaluate your past will cause you to see everything as all bad. Just as no family is perfect, no family is all bad. I know there are some highly dysfunctional families out there (I see them in my office every week), but even within their dysfunction there is usually a little pearl of something positive. And even if your family was one of those highly dysfunctional families, they did not make up all of your history. We also learn about how to be a husband or wife and a parent from other adults we have been exposed to. So if you are having a difficult time finding something positive in your childhood, consider looking at all the role models you were exposed to.

Clear glasses. The final type of glasses you can wear as you evaluate your past is those with no tint at all. The clear lenses allow you to realistically look at your past and see both the good and the not-so-good aspects. From this vantage, point you will be able to process the events of your childhood and young adulthood and see how they have affected the way you view the world and the way you view marriage and parenting. These glasses allow you to accept the negative experiences in your past that you want to learn from and not repeat. They also allow you to balance these negatives by seeing the positive experiences and gleaning from them the traits you would like to see in yourself as you form your own family.

Remember, you choose which glasses you grab when you look into your past. Choose carefully so that you can heal old wounds and continue healthy traditions. The glasses you wear also will affect the expectations you form. (In the next chapter I will discuss the impact that expectations have on your perceived marital satisfaction.)

Realizing What You Learned

You are who you are today because of a variety of unique personal experiences. Your thinking, expectations, beliefs, and worldview have been forming from the day you were born. You have been influenced by your parents and their relationship with you and with each other. They have molded your impressions of marriage and parenting through the ways they lived their own lives. You have also been influenced by the culture and time in which you grew up, the books you read, the movies you saw, and the people you interacted with. You have learned through your own choices and the reactions that those choices evoked from those around you. No wonder no two people are exactly alike; no two histories are exactly alike.

So let's consider just what it is that you have learned from your past. More than you realized, I'm sure. Throughout your life you have learned about

1. male and female roles;
2. the division of labor in and out of the home;
3. who's in charge;
4. ways to show affection (or not);
5. attitudes toward sex;
6. ways to treat the opposite sex;
7. the way you expect to be treated by the opposite sex;
8. ways to handle conflict;
9. forming priorities regarding who or what really comes first;
10. expectations of how children are to act or be raised.

You have been given many examples regarding marriage and parenting, and each of these has had an impact on who you are and what you expect and believe about life. You will either follow the examples set before you, go to the opposite extreme, or openly work to strike a balance and find the healthiest middle ground that will work for you and your family.

Although we may not be aware at the time that we are learning about future relationships, this learning is still powerful. Through this learning process, we often see unhealthy family-of-origin patterns repeated generation after generation. If we do not take time to become aware of what we have learned and how that has influenced our adult relationships, then we are destined to repeat the patterns. Although this may not be a conscious choice, we may still find ourselves right in the middle of what we had hoped not to repeat. If you want to avoid repeating unhealthy patterns, the key is to become aware of these patterns. Without this awareness, you may find yourself repeating old patterns, either because that is all you know how to do (such as continuing in a caretaker or victim role) or because you are trying to redo or fix something that didn't work in childhood (such as by marrying someone just like your father or mother). Regardless of why you are doing it, it is just as unhealthy as when you were a child. But once you become aware that it is not a pattern that you wish to continue, you will have the power to choose a different path.

Another possibility is that you may be aware of something you definitely do not want to repeat in your future relationships and therefore may find yourself going to the opposite extreme. This often results in problems of its own. Take, for example, the father who was spanked excessively or even beaten as a child. He may find himself deciding never to spank or even be involved in the discipline of his children for fear that he will turn out just like his dad. Or consider the mother who, as a child, was never allowed to spend time with friends or go to social events. She may decide to indulge her child in every activity and set no boundaries for activities. Do you see how jumping from one extreme to the other can simply replace one set of problems with a new set?

This process of jumping from one extreme to the other played itself out in my own family of origin and affected me. My mother, the oldest of five children, lived with her mother and stepfather. Both parents worked long hours in the restaurant they owned. Two of her younger brothers had cystic fibrosis and were quite ill at times. In these circumstances, my mom was forced to grow up fairly quickly and by the age of twelve was required to make dinner for the family every evening. Although this may not seem like a huge ordeal, it became a definite sore spot for my mother. Once she was married and started having children of her own, her opposition to her upbringing began to show. She so hated being forced to grow up quickly and be responsible for cooking daily that she, consciously or unconsciously, decided that her children would not have to endure that kind of hardship. And as a result, growing up we were never expected to cook or help cook.

What my mother did out of very positive motives still had a negative impact on me. About four months before I was to get married (that means I was twenty-one years old) my mom realized I did not know how to cook and decided it was time I learned. She came up with this great idea that I would be responsible for one family meal a week. That included planning the menu, shopping for the food, and preparing it. That sounded good to me because at that time all I knew how to cook was macaroni and cheese, scrambled eggs and toast, and frozen pizza. The first week came, and I planned and prepared the meal all by myself. As the family sat down to eat, it was quickly determined that that would be my first and last attempt at cooking while living at home. My mother decided that Jim would get the privilege of teaching me to cook.

Although this may not be an extremely destructive example, you can see that jumping from one extreme to the other can still cause unhealthy experiences in your children. The answer is not to decide just to do the opposite of what your parents did, but instead to take time to evaluate how you can change in order to teach your children something healthier than you were taught.

Acknowledging That It's No Excuse

Regardless of how good or bad your own childhood was, that should play only a small role in how your relationships as an adult turn out. As an adult, you have the freedom and ability to make your own choices. Taking time to consult the rearview mirror is your responsibility. It is also your responsibility to keep your eyes primarily focused on the road ahead and to choose what color glasses you will wear as you travel. This road into your future is one that you pave for yourself—you choose where it is headed.

As children grow up and begin to develop dating relationships, they will often attempt to establish relationships that fit the model they are accustomed to. A boy may be attracted to the girl who lets him continue in his "known" way of behaving. It may not be healthy or happy, but it is a habit. A girl may be attracted to a boy who treats her the same way her father did. Again, maybe not healthy, but habit. If we have not taken time to evaluate our past and determined what kind of person we want to date and marry, then we are likely to make unconscious choices that are unhealthy for us.

Another way that failure to openly evaluate the past may affect you in the future is that you can fool yourself into thinking you are doing so much better than your parents, when maybe that is not really the case. For example, let's say that you grew up with an alcoholic father who was verbally abusive and controlling. You decide that when you are all grown up, you will never drink because you can't stand how your father acted when he was drunk. So you grow up, get married and have children, and never drink. Does that mean you are changing the pattern? Maybe. But if you continue the pattern of being verbally abusive and controlling, regardless of being sober, not much has really changed. You are simply fooling yourself if you think that you are being better than your parents by simply removing the one most painful part of what they did to you. Without consciously evaluating all that your parents did that might have been destructive, you will not be making the most educated and healthy changes for your future.

Dave Carder et al., in the book *Secrets of Your Family Tree,* explain, "The more an individual understands his or her past, the greater the possibility that he or she will be able to control what he or she passes on to the next generation."[1] How true that is. My encouragement to you is that you will actively and consciously take time to review and evaluate your family history with clear glasses on and determine what you do and do not wish to continue in your current relationship and family.

Creating a Healthier Next Generation

The quality of your parents' relationship will influence your thoughts and expectations about marriage and parenting. But it is not the sole determinant of your marital success or failure. You can choose to break unhealthy patterns learned from your family and therefore become a healthier role model for your children.

Here are a few suggestions to help you do this:

1. Understand your past. You must become aware of what your family taught you before you will be able to make changes.

2. Make a choice. You have learned both good and bad traits from your family of origin. Remember, no family is either perfect or all bad. As you evaluate your upbringing, consciously choose which parts you want to carry with you and which you are better off leaving behind. Work to glean what good you can from your role models. Decide what you do and do not want to take with you into your marriage. Where you received a poor example, determine what you want to replace it with.

3. Educate yourself. Learn everything you can about new and healthier ways to interact. This can be done in several ways. You may want to find a mentor couple or small group. Surrounding yourselves with healthy couples can help you develop healthy habits in your own marriage. Observe them, ask questions, and learn from their experiences. You may also choose to learn about healthy relationships through some of the many great books, seminars, conferences, and workshops available today. Use these resources to learn what you can, and start applying what works for the two of you in your marriage.

4. Talk to each other. As you spend time talking, find out what your spouse needs or wants in a marriage partner. Ask what you could do differently or what bad habits you may be demonstrating. Believe me, it is easier to hear this if you have asked rather than if your spouse just decided you need to be told. So open yourself up for some constructive feedback, and begin to make the changes that are needed.

5. Look to God and His Word for the best example of healthy relationships. God has provided us with much information about how to have the best relationships possible. Study what He has to say.

Coming Up Next ...

As you spend time evaluating your history and determining how you are going to view your past, you will soon realize that you have formed many expectations as to what marriage and parenting will be like. These expectations ultimately will influence the level of satisfaction you perceive within marriage. To be as satisfied and happy in your relationship as possible, identify your expectations and learn to express these openly to your spouse. That will be the focus of the next chapter.

CHAPTER TWO

THIS IS NOT WHAT I EXPECTED

Essential Element 2: Expectations

*H*ow do we learn what to expect in marriage? Our perceived satisfaction in current relationships is based on the expectations we developed in childhood and beyond. Whether you feel satisfied in marriage depends largely on what you expected it to be like and how close reality is to that expectation. The closer reality is to what you expected, the greater your feelings of satisfaction. But when reality seems to be a far cry from the picture you had formed in your mind, then you begin to become dissatisfied and unhappy. At that point (if not before) you must take time to evaluate exactly what you were expecting and why it is not happening.

Recognizing Differences

Spending time identifying your family differences and discussing how these may play into your personal expectations will go a long way toward reducing conflicts in the future. One of the most important keys here is to learn that "different" does not mean "wrong." We can become so set in our ways and our family traditions that we begin to believe that our way is the best (or only) way to do something. But once you are married, you soon learn that your spouse is likely thinking the same thing. How can you both be "right"? You can't! Therefore, the logical conclusion becomes, "Then he (or she) must be wrong." Many times, I felt that the way Jim wanted to handle a situation was just flat-out wrong (and I'm sure that at times he felt the same toward me). But in reality it was just different from the way I wanted to handle it. Both of our ideas were formed directly out of how we had seen it done in our homes growing up. The sooner the two of you agree that different is not wrong, the sooner you will be able to openly discuss your family differences and make joint decisions about how you want your family to be.

Jim and I come from very different families with very different ways of doing things. These differences showed up in simple everyday events, habits, and beliefs and often caused conflict between us because we focused on the "right" way to do something. Once we realized there are many ways to do just about anything, we could more easily bring our ideas to the table and decide what seemed to work best for the two of us. Before that, it felt as though we were fighting to be loyal to our families and the way we had always done it. This is not about one family being better or worse than the other; it is about functioning the best you can as a couple.

I remember going to the grocery store by myself early in our marriage and getting a week's worth of groceries. I was pretty proud of myself. (This was not something I had done while living with my parents.) When I got home and was unloading the groceries, Jim grabbed the receipt and reviewed it. He asked why I had not used any coupons. Coupons? What coupons? I never use coupons. Aren't coupons for people who can't afford to pay regular prices for their food? I could afford to buy food, couldn't I? Besides, where was I going to get coupons? I was beginning to worry that we were broke (which we were, but I just didn't know it) and that Jim was looking at the receipt because he was angry and thought I had spent too much money. Here I thought he would be proud of me for doing the shopping so he would not have to worry about it. Instead, my head was seeing visions of us living on the streets in rags and cardboard boxes.

Jim explained that he believed it was a wise use of our money to clip coupons and save money whenever we could. His mother had always been a smart shopper, and he grew up watching her compare ads, clip and use coupons, and buy on-sale items they might need in the near future. To Jim, the idea of going to the grocery store without having compared the ads and sorted coupons was simply irresponsible. To me? Well, it never even crossed my mind. I do not remember my mom using coupons, but then I seldom went shopping with her. I had just formed my own opinion, and it obviously did not match my husband's expectation that we would use coupons.

Once we talked this through and I did not feel as though he were telling me I was wrong, and he did not feel as though I were telling him that his family couldn't afford to shop without coupons, we were able to decide what was best for our newly formed family. Coupons became beneficial to me once Jim explained to me that yes, we could afford to buy our food, but since we were poor graduate students, if we did not use coupons, we would not be able to afford our date night. All of a sudden I became one of the smartest shoppers ever. I quickly acquired a marvelous collection of coupons that were neatly organized in their own little holder. Date nights began to mean even more to me because I knew we had to work to make them happen.

As you can see, expectations can affect just about any area of marriage. The expectations we have formed are not only about married life, but also about issues regarding children and parenting. Some of these expectations hit us right between the eyes as soon as we get married. These are usually the ones that have to do specifically with our views of husband and wife roles and responsibilities. As you work through these in the early stages of marriage, you may come to think you have dealt with all your expectations and no longer really have to be concerned with them. But this is not the case. You have also formed expectations that have to do with parenting issues and how best to raise your children. They may not show up until much later in your relationship. Never stop taking time to evaluate where you may have unspoken expectations you need to address.

Trying to Work It Out

Jim and I had our first child when we had been married for six years. Although we very much wanted to be parents, we had no idea what this little bundle of joy would bring with her. As I shared earlier, our upbringings were very different and had been the source of many conversations, discussions, and arguments during the early years of our marriage. We had spent countless hours facing our different expectations about marriage and had worked to blend the best of both of our histories into what we felt was a good working relationship. We were sure we had figured out all we needed to in regard to how our past was affecting our present. But we were sorely mistaken. When Taffeta entered the scene (and ever since), our different views of the world once again took center stage.

We soon realized that we had a whole set of expectations we had never noticed, let alone discussed. How we were going to raise our children and how we would relate to each other as parents became the topic of many conversations. We each knew how we had been raised and were sure that was the best and only way to do it. We discussed current issues, such as whether or not to breastfeed and if and when I would go back to work. We also discussed future issues, such as how much (if any) allowance to give and whether we would buy our kids cars when they turned sixteen. We seemed to disagree on practically everything.

The past eleven years have consisted of many discussions and just as many opportunities for compromise. We still do not have all of these issues figured out (I still have a few years to work on him about the car-at-sixteen thing), but we have made some major headway and will continue to address the issues as they arise. Remembering to apply the belief that "different" does not mean "wrong" has helped us on many occasions to get past the right-vs.-wrong way of doing things and reach a decision as a couple as to what works best for our family.

Many couples I counsel struggle with this issue of expectations. When they come to see me, they almost always share feelings of dissatisfaction with their marriage. When we get right down to it, much of this dissatisfaction has to do with unmet expectations.

Understanding Unmet Expectations

If expectations are so vital to the health of marriages, why are they going unmet in most marriages? You may experience unmet expectations within marriage for three possible reasons. The first is that you have never informed each other of your expectations. How can you meet a need or comply with a rule that you do not even know exists? Many couples begin their lives together with stars in their eyes and thoughts focused on the wedding or honeymoon plans. They spend hours and hours planning the details of what color the cummerbunds should be or which cake topper to choose. In this process, they often miss putting time into planning the most important part of the wedding—the marriage. Couples spend virtually no time discussing their expectations of what life together will be like. Even after years of marriage, we find that most couples are not very good at identifying and discussing their past, present, or future expectations. Disappointments will happen if you do not both know what you expect from yourselves and each other. Have the two of you sat down and asked each other questions that would help you identify and share your expectations? For example, before you got married, or at least early in your marriage, did you discuss

1. if and when you wanted to have children and how many?
2. career choices or desires for each of you?
3. division of labor before and after children?
4. how often to take vacations?

These are just a few of the things about which people hold expectations that they do not discuss until a conflict arises. Some of these may not seem like big, make-it-or-break-it topics, but they can end up being just that. Any time you have an expectation you have not talked about together, you have an opportunity for disappointment and conflict. The more you can openly identify and discuss your expectations, the more likely your spouse will be able to meet them.

The second possible reason that expectations are not met is that they may be unrealistic. Even if you openly voice your expectations, there are going to be some that your spouse is simply unable to meet. Many spouses would happily meet the other's needs if they knew what they were and if they were capable of doing so. However, we often want a spouse to do things for us or to take on a role that is completely unrealistic. It is important to note here that many couples hold unrealistic expectations not only of each other but also of the impact of adding children into the mix. Again, if these unrealistic expectations are not identified and adjusted before you have children, you may find yourselves disappointed after the children arrive. (More on unrealistic expectations regarding children in the next section.)

The final reason some of our expectations may go unmet is the most destructive of the three. This reason involves your spouse *not wanting* to meet your expectations for him or her or for your marriage. If you openly state your expectations, and the two of you evaluate them and consider them to be realistic expectations for your relationship and your family, then you should be able to look forward to those expectations being met, at least most of the time. If these realistic expectations are not being met, there may be a deeper issue to be addressed. This type of situation would most likely be best dealt with through professional counseling.

I hope you now have a better understanding of how expectations can have a major influence on your level of happiness and satisfaction within your marriage, and why you may have unmet expectations. Now let's look at some of the more commonly held unrealistic expectations or beliefs about adding children into the marital mix. If your expectations are unrealistic, then you can assume that dissatisfaction and unhappiness will be the result if you fail to adjust those expectations.

Five Crazy Beliefs about Children

1. Our marital relationship won't change all that much. Yeah, right! Oh, if only that were the case. The relationship will begin to change the moment you seriously decide you are ready to have children (or the moment you find out you are pregnant, for those who did not "decide"). These changes start in the mind. You begin to think differently about yourself, your spouse, and your responsibilities. You start to look at your spouse as a dad or mom. You start to consider what raising a child will mean. Will I have to work longer hours? Will I quit my job and stay home? We'd better start saving money now. And on and on the thoughts race. And once the mindset begins to change, everything else follows.

Where you spend your money, time, and energy begins to change even before the baby arrives. These changes continue and intensify once the child is here and for the next eighteen or more years. How you talk to each other and spend time with each other will never be the same again. (We'll say more about these changes in part 2.)

2. Having a baby will draw us closer together. If research means anything, this will not be the case. Multiple research studies say that marital satisfaction plummets after the birth of the first child.[1] The challenges of a new baby, new roles, new expectations, and new needs can all become overwhelming to the new parents. Then add in being so tired that you cannot even consider having a conversation to discuss all these changes in hopes, wants, and needs. This is the making of a couple of people who once were in love and now barely recognize each other. Their feelings of connectedness and closeness have been replaced (at least temporarily) with cries and conflicts. They may know that their love for each other is still there, somewhere, buried beneath a pile of diapers, bottles, squeaky toys, and unopened mail, but finding it right now seems an impossible task.

Although over the next few years, children do grow and begin to take care of some of their own basic needs, the couple's time together may never be the same. Couples who realize the need to make time for each other will do better than most. But even they will need to make some adjustments in the ways they stay connected.

3. Having a child will solve all our problems. So many couples today decide to have children for all the wrong reasons. They believe that having kids will bring an end to all the pain in their lives. Somehow the home will magically become filled with love and warmth when they bring the baby through the door. They somehow hold on to the belief that the addition of children into the marital mix will serve as a way to solve problems that the marital relationship may be having. This belief is based on the idea that once we have a baby, everything good will only get better and everything bad will disappear. Actually, the opposite is true; a baby often makes things worse. If the couple does not deal with the problems they already were having, the problems will most likely rear their ugly heads again. Why? Because unresolved conflict always shows back up. And now you will be sleep-deprived and cranky when it gets there and even less likely to resolve it with a baby crying in the background.

4. Having a child will meet all my needs and make me whole. When we view children as the way to complete ourselves, what are we really saying? We seem to be saying that we are not complete individuals on our own and we need someone to make up for what we cannot do. This unrealistic expectation is strongly tied to personal struggles of low self-esteem and feelings of inferiority. (See chapter 3 for help with self-esteem issues.) We would do much better to work first on our own self-esteem and learn to accept who we are. Once we are content and comfortable with who we are, then we will not need someone else to make us whole. We will be able to have children and allow them to become the people God created them to be, without trying to make them fill in our gaps.

Furthermore, if you believe that a child is going to meet your needs, you are going to be sorely disappointed. The needs I most often hear soon-to-be-parents say they expect a child will fill are the need to be loved unconditionally and the need to be needed. Experiences of caring for our new baby early on may make us feel needed and important. However, as we realize that these demands are a constant drain and that we rarely get a break, we begin to feel suffocated. Unconditional love is something that we spend our entire lives learning to give. How could we expect a new baby or young child to love us unconditionally?

5. My child will be just like me. This belief is based on the idea that "my way is the best way." You expect that of course your children will think, feel, and act the way you do. That would only make sense. Everyone wants to do things the best way, don't they? And since you and your children are going to think, feel, and act the same way, then of course you will end up being the best of friends. Right? Wrong! At least not as they are growing up. The friendship you have with your children is something that develops as you move into an adult relationship with them. Before that, your job is to be a parent first and foremost. And because you will be parenting, there may be many times where you find you really do not like each other much at all.

We are all unique, God-created individuals with our own thoughts, feelings, and beliefs. We must learn to identify and appreciate our differences. In accepting these differences, we have the opportunity to grow toward greater intimacy. And, even if your child *is* "just like you" in many ways, once he or she becomes a teenager (or maybe sooner) your child will actively work to be not like you. Children need and want to be their own persons. And part of their development is to individuate and develop their own sense of self. That comes out of *proving* they are different from their parents. Let me personalize this for you through a story.

On March 9, 1998, my identical twin was born—a mere thirty years late. The day I gave birth to Tiara was both traumatic and joyful. One of the things I remember most, among the near-death experiences and the looks of relief and joy from everyone in the room when she let out her first cry, was my mother's response to seeing her. In the recovery room, as my family filed in to see our newest addition, my mom stopped dead in her tracks and gasped when she looked down at this precious baby. There were tears in her eyes as she picked her up and said, "Oh, my goodness ... my little Debbie!" She shared that she had always wondered if she could really remember what her babies looked like or if that was just preserved in photos. But that day she knew for sure that she actually did remember as she sat there with goose bumps, holding this little wonder.

It was evident from day one (at least to my mom) that Tiara was the spit and image of me. As she grew, the similarities became so evident to everyone around us that it was almost spooky. What was even more amazing was that Tiara was not simply just like me physically, but she seemed to be just like me from the inside out. The way she would smile or cut her eyes at someone would send my mom running for the photo albums to show me how I used to make that exact same face—and she was right.

Without knowing anything about me as a child, Tiara

☞ became interested in the same things (rainbows and horses)

☞ had the same favorite color (purple) and had to have her room painted in it

☞ showed the same dramatic reaction to the world around her (the same scream and number of tears were required for a hangnail as a broken bone)

☞ became a hopeless hypochondriac (yes, I am embarrassed to admit it, but that was me)

With all these similarities and more, if anyone had reason to believe that "my child will be just like me," it would be me. It began to look as though I was going to get the chance to raise myself—what a weird thought. However, it was not long before Tiara was old enough to understand that being called "Little Debbie" meant she was acting just like her mom. And it then became her job to rebel against that concept. She wanted to be her own person. She would often yell, "Don't call me Little Debbie!" And whenever she found out she was doing something the same way I did, she would do her best to change it. For example, it was only after she had her room painted purple and more than half of her wardrobe in the same color that she found out purple had been my favorite color when I was young. I had also had my room decorated in purple. That is all it took for her to pick a new favorite color and start making plans for her next room to be blue. We have not had the heart to tell her that my next room and favorite color was none other than—you guessed it—blue. Poor thing, even as she fights this, it seems to keep haunting her.

If you think your child is going to be just like you, think again. No matter how much they really are like you, children will do their best to become their own persons. That is just part of their development, and it is healthy for them to exert their own sense of self. Whether they start differentiating before the age of eight or wait until they are teenagers, they will attempt to prove that they are different from you. Get ready for it. Now that I think about it, maybe I can use Tiara's strong desire to be different from me to my advantage. By the time she is a teenager, I could tell her that I was a horribly rebellious child who disobeyed her parents and did all sorts of bad things. Maybe she will have to prove that she is not like me and become one of those obedient, compliant teens. That just might work. I'll let you know.

Wrapping It Up

Regardless of which stage of marriage and parenting you are in, take time to identify and work through as many of these little (and big) differences as you possibly can. Some of the major areas that you may want to review for personal differences would include

- management of family finances;
- marital roles;
- division of labor around the house;
- holiday and birthday traditions;
- religious preferences and beliefs.

Some of the major areas of parenting that you may want to discuss would include

- types of discipline;
- number and timing of children;
- marital roles and division of labor changes;
- responsibilities for children;
- childcare options;
- whether to buy children cars when they turn sixteen (let me know what you figure out on this one, since we still have not reached a solution).

Coming Up Next ...

You now understand the impact that your past and your expectations can have on your marriage. But what about the impact of self-esteem? Can your view of yourself really affect those around you? Can you love others even if you do not really love yourself? The answers may surprise you. So, if you really want to know, just turn the page.

CHAPTER THREE

HOW MUCH DO I LIKE *ME*?

Essential Element 3: Positive Self-esteem

*D*o not adjust your reading glasses! You did read what you just thought you read. Yes, the title of this chapter is How Much Do I Like *Me*? Are you surprised to see a whole chapter in a marriage book devoted to liking yourself? If you keep reading, very soon you will understand why this is such an important chapter and one I hope you do not decide to skip. This very well may be the most challenging chapter, and I urge you to stay with me and read it through to completion because one of the most essential elements of building a strong marriage and family is having a healthy view of oneself.

Giving What You Do Not Possess?

You cannot give what you do not possess. Do you believe that statement? One weekend, I was speaking to a group of women who were shivering with cold. The hotel's thermostat was not working properly, and the conference room felt like the inside of a refrigerator. We suffered through it for the first evening. The next morning as I was speaking, I noticed one ingenious lady wrapped up snugly in a nice warm blanket she had brought from her car. I asked to borrow her blanket just for a moment. She hesitated only slightly before unwrapping and handing it over. Once I had the coveted blanket, I held it up to the rest of the teeth-chattering crowd and said, "I would like to auction off this toasty warm blanket to the highest bidder. Do I have any takers?" Although just about every woman in that room would have loved to have that blanket, no one made a bid. I questioned them, "Ah, come on. Surely someone wants this; I can tell you're all freezing. Why isn't anyone bidding?" And from the back of the room I heard one lady say, "You have no right to offer that blanket to us; it's not yours to give." BINGO! It was not mine to give. I did not own it. And even if someone in the room had made a bid on the blanket, she never would have received it because I never had it to give. Think of the disappointment that would have caused—and I'm sure my speaker-evaluation scores would have taken a dramatic dip.

Now let me ask you again, do you believe in this statement: You cannot give what you do not possess? A marriage is based on love, commitment, and acceptance of each other. How can you learn to love and accept another person if you do not first know how to love and accept yourself? Offering to give something you do not possess will only leave those expecting to receive it feeling empty and disappointed. This applies not only to our possessions but also to the love we have to give. If you struggle with loving yourself, be prepared for your spouse and your children to struggle to feel love from you. You can give away only as much love as you already possess for yourself.

Why is it that we Christians seem to have such a hard time loving ourselves? Why do we struggle to feel valuable to ourselves, each other, and even to God? I heard a wonderful illustration that drives this point home. As the speaker began his speech, he held up a brand-new, crisp twenty-dollar bill and asked who wanted it. All the people in the room raised their hands. He smiled and said, "Okay, but wait just a minute. I need to do something first." He proceeded to fold the brand new, perfect bill in half. After he made sure the crease was good and evident, he folded it again and creased it. He repeated this several times, then unfolded the twenty-dollar bill, which could no longer stay perfectly straight. He then asked who in the audience wanted the twenty dollars now. All the same hands flew up into the air. He held up his hand, signaling for the crowd to wait once again, and he wadded the money up into a tight ball. This time when he tried to unfold it, the twenty-dollar bill tore slightly and was thoroughly wrinkled and disfigured. But when he asked the audience if they still wanted it, they did. Finally, the speaker took the money and dropped it to the floor and began to stomp on it. He twisted his foot back and forth, grinding the paper into the floor. When he held up the twenty-dollar bill this time, it hardly looked like what it had been just a few moments before. It was now crumpled, torn, and dirty. But even with the bill in that awful state, the entire audience raised their hands to indicate they wanted it. Why do you think that was? Of course we all know it was because the value of that twenty-dollar bill never changed, no matter what it went through.

What a powerful illustration about self-esteem and personal value. How many of us see ourselves like that twenty-dollar bill? We are born neat and clean and valuable, but over the years life takes its toll, and as things happen to us or we suffer the consequences of our own poor choices, we begin to feel like old dirty rags that are of no value to anyone. But God sees our real value—the events of life do not change our value to Him and should not change our value to each other.

Giving Yourself a Grade

Before moving on, take a couple of minutes right now and honestly evaluate yourself. How do you really feel about yourself? This should be an overall assessment. Consider your whole self—physical condition, appearance, personality, spiritual state, talent, intellect. Everything. Based on this evaluation, give yourself a grade: A, B, C, D, or F (you can even put in + or −). Be honest about how you feel about yourself—not how you think you *should* feel or how others view you. This is just for you; no one else will see it. Now grab a small piece of paper, write your grade on it, fold it, and stick it in this book for later. Do this before continuing to read. I promise to come back to this before the end of the chapter.

Now that you have completed that little assignment, I want you to imagine yourself in this story. You are a college art professor. You have spent almost a whole year with this particular group of talented students. Actually, you have decided that this has been the best group of students you have worked with in all your years of teaching. It has been an enjoyable year for you as you have watched your students' talents improve, and you are a little sad to see it coming to an end. You have taken them through several modes of expressing their art—sketching, painting, pottery, sculpture, and so forth. But now it's time to show what they can really do—it's finals.

You give the final assignment, which is to reach as deep as they can inside themselves and create their best work yet. You encourage them by reminding them of all the wonderful things they have created throughout the year. At the same time, you challenge them by saying that you know they have something even better down deep inside themselves. And that is what you want them to create for their final grade. You give no other instructions. Your students have total freedom. They are nervous at the lack of structure and unsure whether they can meet your expectations. But you anxiously anticipate what wonders you are going to see, especially from your star pupil. He had "wowed" you all year with the amazing things he created, and you knew that his was a true talent. His name is ... God. And you just know He's going to do something really big someday.

Then the grading day finally arrives. You walk around the room admiring your students' work and handing out the grades. Overall, you are pleased with the work, but you really can't wait to see what your star student—God—has created. The time finally arrives for God to unveil what He reached down deep inside Himself to find. The cover is removed and there you are looking right in the eyes of God's greatest creation. Guess what it is? *You!*

Now it is time to give God His grade. Find that little piece of paper you stuck in the book just a few moments ago. Open it and give God the grade you believe He deserves on His creation.

Is that really the grade He deserves? Unless it is an A+, the answer is no.

Every time we cut ourselves down, think badly of ourselves, or fail to take care of ourselves, we in essence tell God that we do not like what He made. We are saying, "Hey, God, what'd You do, just throw this thing together at the last minute? I think You could have done better."

But God did not think He could do better. He knew He had created many things, but He had not created His best yet. After five days of creating the universe and everything in it, God spent day six (finals) reaching down deep inside Himself and creating the very best He could. Let's look at what God had to say about what He created. When we review the week of creation, we see that God evaluated His work several times:

- ☞ After making the light ... He saw it was good (Gen. 1:4)
- ☞ After making the land and sea ... He saw it was good (1:10)
- ☞ After making the plants and trees ... He saw it was good (1:12)

☞ After making the sun, moon, and stars ... He
saw it was good (1:18)

☞ After making the fish and the birds ... He saw
it was good (1:21)

☞ After making the animals ...He saw it was
good (1:25)

On the sixth day, God created humans. And at the end of that day, when God evaluated all His work, do you know what He said? He said, "It was *very* good!" (1:31, emphasis added).

Why not brag? God did! Review the verses above. After God did something, He stepped back, evaluated it, and gave Himself a compliment: "It is good!" He gave Himself an A! Then He gave Himself an A+ after He created humans. Wow! God thinks we are A+ material.

Psalm 139:14 declares that we are "fearfully and wonderfully made" and that the works of God's hands are wonderful. And we are the works of His hands. What do you think of when you think of the works of someone's hands? I think of some of the handmade gifts I have received from people I love. I have many treasures around my home, but one especially stands out. I have a beautiful, hand-knitted baby afghan that my grandmother made at the birth of my first child. I am sure many of you have similar treasures. How did you feel when you received that handmade gift? I felt extremely loved and touched that my grandmother would take her time to make this for me with her own hands. I have thanked her more than once and have always treasured it. I keep it in a safe place, and when the kids pull out every blanket and sheet in the house to make tunnels and tents, I do not allow them to use this one. It is much too special, and I would hate to see anything bad happen to it. So I protect it.

But let's say that one day my grandma comes to my house for a surprise visit. When she walks into the living room, she sees that beautiful afghan on the floor with our two new puppies lying on it. How do you think that would make her feel? Crushed would be an understatement, I'm sure.

There is someone else who knitted something for me even more special than this—let me show you. Psalm 139:13 says, "For you created my inmost being; you knit me together in my mother's womb." My God took the time to knit me together in my mother's womb. And He knitted you together—can you picture that? We are "handmade"! Just think of the love and effort He put into making you. Wow!

Now think of how it must grieve God when we do not treasure and love what He handmade. Can you imagine how it must hurt Him to have His creation say, "I don't like what you made, God. It doesn't mean all that much to me. As a matter of fact, instead of taking care of it and protecting it, I think I'll just throw it to the dogs." Or maybe we do tell Him with our *words* that we like what He made but then do not show it with our *actions*. We may be able to say that God did a good job when He made us, but then we let ourselves go to waste. Maybe we do not take care of ourselves physically, emotionally, or spiritually. Maybe we do not use the talents and gifts He gave us when He knit us together. It is like telling my grandmother that I like what she made but then not taking care of it or using it for what she intended. It was made for a special purpose—and so were you. Saying God did well in creating you but then not fulfilling your purpose, not using your talents, or not taking care of yourself shows that you do not value what He made. Either way, God is not getting the glory He deserves for His creation. How this must hurt Him, especially when He knows He took the time to knit you together in your mother's womb and to count the hairs on your head. Oh, how we must grieve Him when we do not love ourselves.

Being Imitators of God

God liked what He made. And the Bible says in Ephesians 5:1, "Be imitators of God." So if we are to imitate God, then I think that means we should also like what He made. The Bible also teaches that we are expected to praise God (Ps. 103:20–22; Ps. 113:1–3; Ps. 150:6) and that we should praise Him for the works of His hands (Ps. 92:1–5; Ps. 138:1–2; Heb. 13:15). God expects me to praise Him for the things He has done and the things He has made. I do not think anyone will argue that point. If I can stand on a mountaintop looking out over creation and praise God for the beauty of nature, how much more should I be able to praise Him for what He Himself identified as His greatest creation—us?

When you look at yourself, do you like what you see? Do you praise God for what He made in you? Can you make a list of things you like about yourself? If not, why not? I am saddened by the number of Christians I encounter who cannot do this simple assignment. As a matter of fact, when I ask people in my office to make a list of wonderful things about themselves, they react as if I am asking them to commit a grievous sin. Many Christians have come to the conclusion that it is wrong to love themselves and even more wrong to openly identify what they might like about themselves if they were allowed to like themselves. Heaven forbid they might brag! What is so wrong with being able to have a healthy sense of who you are and being able to openly acknowledge that you love yourself? Not only is loving yourself *not* a sin, it is actually a commandment of our Lord Jesus Christ! Now how's that for power? Let's look at a Scripture passage and see what Jesus has to say about loving ourselves.

In Matthew 22 the religious teachers of the time were attempting to test Jesus. They asked Him which commandment is the greatest.

> Jesus replied: "'Love the Lord your God with all your
> heart and with all your soul and with all your mind.' This
> is the first and greatest commandment. And the second is
> like it: 'Love your neighbor as yourself.'"
> —Matthew 22:37–39

There it is, a little two-letter word that many of us have chosen to overlook: *as.* We seem to just read "love your neighbor," and we are pretty good at doing that. As a matter of fact, we even believe we are to love our enemies. So if we can love our neighbors and our enemies—why not ourselves? Are we less worthy than our enemy? Some of you may truly think so, but I'm here to tell you that is a lie direct from the pit of hell! The Bible says we are to love our neighbor *as* ourselves. That sounds to me as though if you do not love yourself, your neighbor has a problem, especially those "neighbors" closest to you, such as your spouse and your children.

Learning to identify the things about yourself that you like is the first step in learning to love yourself. Now think again and try to come up with a list of things you like about yourself. Remember, there is nothing wrong with doing this. This is simply giving credit where credit is due. I can say I like my eyes because I did not have anything to do with making them look like this. I can say I like writing books, because I didn't give myself that talent or the intellect to do it. Identifying the positive things about myself should be nothing more than one more way to glorify my God. It is my way of saying I like the works of His hands. It is giving God an A+.

Believing that God really did make something wonderful in us is only the first step. We must then evaluate whether our actions are showing that we believe that. Are your actions showing that you treasure what God created in you? Let's see.

Having Nothing Left to Give

People, especially women and moms, often fall into the trap of giving to and caring for everyone else, then maybe if there is any time or energy left over—which there seldom is—they might do something for themselves. If you fall into this category, you need to understand how giving everything you have to everyone else leaves nothing for you to give to yourself. This process will actually begin a negative spiral that will end in feelings of worthlessness and low self-esteem.

To start this evaluation, ask yourself this question: What are some of the things you do for yourself? Take a minute and really think about this. In the past week or so, what have you taken time to do just for you? Many of you may have to say, "Nothing." And if that is your answer, you may be in a very dangerous place in your life. Let me show you what happens when you do nothing for yourself. Nothing begets nothing.

If you *do* nothing for yourself, you will *think* nothing of yourself. Then you *feel* like nothing.

And this can happen in reverse: If you *feel* like a great big nothing, you will *think* nothing of yourself, and you will *do* nothing for yourself.

And the cycle goes on and on and on. If you are in one of these spirals, you can change it!

So how do you break this cycle? How do you stop *feeling* like a great big nothing and start feeling like a somebody? Sometimes feelings just seem so powerful and overwhelming that we feel controlled by them. But I am here to tell you there is hope. There is a way to stop being controlled by how you feel and start understanding that you can control those overwhelming feelings.

God understands that our feelings are real and often very strong. He also knows, however, that feelings never stand alone. In Luke 12:34, Jesus gave us the key to understanding and controlling our feelings when He said, "Where your treasure is, there your heart will be also." Let's take some time to break this verse down to better understand it.

What does it mean to "treasure" something? You show that you treasure something by the way you think and act toward it. The more of your time and energy you give to something, the more evident it is that you consider it to be of high value. When you treasure something, you will not only treat it well, you will also think about it often and in a very positive way. You would not view something as a treasure and then think awful things about it. According to this verse, "where your treasure is" would therefore refer to where you are placing your time, energy, and thoughts.

"There your heart will be." The "heart" here does not refer to the physical heart, but rather to the inner self—our feelings and emotions. So if we put this all together, what do we get? "Where your treasure is, there your heart will be," loosely paraphrased by Debbie, becomes something like, "The more positive time and energy you devote to something, the more positive you are going to feel about it." God knows that our feelings change and are a result of the thoughts and behaviors that come first. When you put all your time, energy, and thoughts into what other people need from you, you are treasuring them. But what does that say about you? If you put *no* time, energy, or positive thoughts into yourself, then you definitely are *not* treasuring yourself. To treasure what God made in you and to start liking who you are, you must start investing time and energy and positive thoughts into yourself. Knowing how to balance what you give to others and how you give and take care of yourself is essential to a positive sense of self-worth. When you understand that feelings are the result of thoughts and behaviors, you will realize that to feel like a somebody, you must act and think like you are a somebody. Stop giving yourself only the leftovers and learn to set aside time just for you on a regular basis.

Improving Your Self-esteem

We are all God-created, and therefore we all have good qualities. Many people, however, struggle with seeing the positive traits in themselves. Instead, they only see ugliness and negative aspects of who they are. These people do not like what they see when they look in the mirror. They struggle with low self-esteem, and this can be destructive not only to the people themselves, but also to their relationships—especially marriages.

People with low self-esteem may have such a hard time seeing positive traits in themselves that they reach the point of believing there is nothing good about themselves. As a result of not liking themselves, they begin to believe that no one else could possibly like them, either. This causes increased tension in a marital relationship, because the person who feels this way not only cannot give the love he or she needs to give but also cannot receive the love offered.

If you are struggling with low self-esteem, make it your number one priority to work on this first. In appendix A, you will find "Ten Steps to Building Your Self-esteem" that will provide you with a few suggestions to get started.

Coming Up Next ...

Once you have learned to treasure yourself, you can then truly begin to treasure those closest to you. Learning the specific ways to act and think about your spouse that will keep the two of you "in love" forever is the focus of the next chapter. You are about to learn how to TREASURE your spouse.

CHAPTER FOUR

HOW DO YOU
KNOW THAT I
LIKE YOU?

Essential Element 4: Treasuring Your Spouse

hink of something that you genuinely treasure—an object you consider to be of great value. Got it? Now if I spent some time with you, how would I know you treasure that object? What would I observe about how you act toward it? If you were hanging out around my house, you would soon notice the things that I treasure, such as my Coca-Cola collection. How would you know I really like my Coke stuff? For starters, it is displayed all over my kitchen. Everywhere you turn you are face to face with some symbol of my favorite soft drink. And just in case you did not notice some of it, I would be sure to point it out to you.

Even within this collection, you would notice that I treasure some pieces more than others because of where I have placed them. There are those pieces that I actually use on a daily basis. Then there are the items set high on a shelf or behind glass that are there for looking at but not touching.

As you observed me and my house, you would be able to tell by my actions—how I display and care for these objects and how I talk about them—that they are valuable to me, that I treasure them. I am sure there are things in your life that you treasure. Maybe it is your car, your house, a medal or a trophy, or any other sentimental or personally valuable item. How do you act toward it? Do you take special care of it? Display it openly and in a safe place?

Now I would like you to consider a person who is valuable and important to you. (The right answer here is your spouse.) If I were hanging out around the two of you, would I be able to tell by the way you treat your spouse that you treasure him or her? Or do you take better care of your possessions than of the people you love? It is essential that the people we love know they are more important to us than any of the things we own. Unfortunately this is not always the case. So just how do we go about showing those people closest to us that we love them? I plan to spend this chapter teaching you to do this through the process of learning how to TREASURE your spouse.

TREASURE-ing Your Spouse

As time passes in a marriage, the newness wears off and the many responsibilities of your lives take over. You start taking your spouse for granted. This is especially easy to do once children arrive on the scene. Treasuring takes time, and time seems to be in very short supply during the parenting stage of our lives. (More on making time for each other in the next chapter.) Regardless of how much or how little time you feel you have, learn to use that time to make your spouse feel treasured. Learn what it means to truly treasure your spouse, and start applying these skills immediately. Let's break down treasuring into its components and then discuss each of these.

TREASURE

T: Thinking positively
R: Respecting
E: Enjoying
A: Attending
S: Shielding
U: Understanding
R: Romancing
E: Edifying

T
Thinking positively

Finally, brothers, whatever is true, whatever is noble,
whatever is right, whatever is pure, whatever is lovely,
whatever is admirable—
if anything is excellent or praiseworthy—
think about such things.

—Philippians 4:8

Consider that you are a part of a sports team, but all you seem to be able to think about are the negative aspects of your teammates. How close do you think you are going to feel to that team? How much of yourself are you really going to invest in that team? How much time, energy, or attention are you going to give? The answer to each of these questions is, "Not much!" The truth may be that your team is not really all bad, but if you focus on the negative, eventually that is what you are going to believe. And if you begin to believe that you are part of an "all bad" team, you will start considering your options of leaving this team and maybe looking for a new team that deserves you more.

If you are going to treasure your spouse, focus your thoughts on his or her positive traits and strengths. Treasuring also involves selectively ignoring the negative characteristics and weaknesses of your spouse. God tells us in Philippians 4:8 to keep our thoughts on things that are pure, lovely, and admirable. At no point do I see Him telling us to think on the negative, ugly, and irritating. Therefore, it would seem that He wants us to actively avoid thinking about things that are negative. If we apply this, we will increase our level of happiness within the marriage. Research shows that "happy couples are couples that accentuate the partner's good traits and motives as causes of his or her positive behavior; his/her negative behavior is seen as rare and unintentional or situational. The happy spouse, thereby, reinforces his/her partner's good traits. In contrast, unhappy couples overlook the positive and emphasize the partner's bad personality traits and negative attitudes as the causes of marital problems."[1]

R
Respecting your spouse

Show proper respect to everyone.
—1 Peter 2:17

Webster's dictionary defines respect in the following manner: "to hold in high esteem, honor, or reverence; to treat with consideration."[2] Wow, what a definition. Showing respect for your spouse means giving the absolute best part of yourself—the best of your attitude, your time, your language, your dress, your gifts, the best everything. Often our spouses end up getting our leftovers, not our best. Be sure your spouse gets your best. Hold him or her in high esteem. Show respect in all you say and do every day. Be sure that the way you talk to or about your spouse is honoring and considerate. It is especially important to show your spouse respect in front of the children. Children learn how to respect others by watching how you respect each other. Don't use hurtful or rough language with your spouse, and don't tease about sensitive topics. Show respect for your spouse's needs for both individuality and togetherness, and help to keep these balanced.

Also show respect for each other's differences. We each are unique and will have different thoughts, beliefs, and ways of doing things. Discuss these differences so that you can better understand what your spouse needs. Openly discuss these issues and share what you are comfortable with and what you are not comfortable with. One way of showing respect to each other would be to agree not to discipline your children in any way that would make your spouse uncomfortable.

E
Enjoying your spouse

> May your fountain be blessed, and may you rejoice
> in the wife [husband] of your youth.
> —Proverbs 5:18

Do you think it would be important for a team of individuals to like each other? Is that a necessary part of a well-functioning team? I think it is. The smaller the team, the closer they need to be to work well together. Since the marriage team has just two people, the importance of enjoying each other is accentuated. This is where being best friends with your spouse helps. As you build the friendship part of your relationship, your team becomes stronger and more stable. How do you build an ever-growing friendship with your spouse? By actively setting aside time to be together and protecting these times. Don't hesitate to pencil your spouse in to your daily calendar. After all, you put all your other important meetings and appointments in there. Fill your time together with talking, laughing, and playing. Work to find specific recreational activities that you both enjoy, and then do them. This will go miles in helping you feel connected.

Pleasure and laughter build a foundation of emotional safety, which is essential to a marriage. Focus on finding pleasure in all that you do. It is always more fun to do whatever you have to do with your best friend. So why not start today? Do anything you possibly can together. You can make even the mundane and routine activities a little more fun if you do them together. Wash the dishes together and put bubbles on her nose or grab hands in the water. Have a pillow fight before making the bed. Rake the leaves and then jump in. Be sure to find fun and laughter everywhere you can.

A
Attending to your spouse

Guard what has been entrusted to your care.
—1 Timothy 6:20

For a team to work well together, the members must pay attention to each other and to how the team works. They can't just *say* that being part of the team is important and then not show up for practice. The marriage team also requires that the members attend to each other. Ah! The amazing power of attention! We all need and want it. We will do just about anything to get it. And the very best kind of all, the undivided kind, is in limited supply. Attention includes giving your time and energy (physically, mentally, and emotionally) to what is important to you. If you want your spouse to feel treasured, then give your undivided attention whenever possible and make him or her a priority in your life. Take a little time out of every day to connect with each other. Even ten or fifteen minutes can make a world of difference if you give each other undivided attention.

As you realize the importance of giving your spouse your attention, it is important to understand that you have two types of attention available to give. There is positive attention and negative attention. Whatever you attend to (either positively or negatively) will be reinforced. If you give your spouse positive attention (hugs; thank-yous; time to cuddle, to talk, or to play together), you will reinforce positive interactions. However, if you give negative attention to your spouse (nagging, fighting, and cutting comments), you will be reinforcing negative interactions, which will likely continue between the two of you. To treasure your spouse, give as much positive attention as you can. This will meet a basic need and strengthen and reinforce the positive interactions within the marriage.

S
Shielding your spouse

[Love] always protects ...
—1 Corinthians 13:7

Showing the members of your team how important they are to you and how much you treasure them includes some form of protection. Can shielding and protecting one of your teammates really be that important? Yes, it can. Without proper protection when and where it's needed, a team can't progress in the game. Being a big football fan, I have spent many hours yelling at the television when a group of men weren't doing their job of protecting their teammates. I have seen games won and lost simply based on one team's ability or inability to protect its quarterback. Understanding the value of protecting your teammates will help them feel treasured and important. Does your spouse deserve any less? Offering protection within marriage may mean providing adequate housing and a safe car to drive. It may mean standing up against those who may be cutting your spouse down (even within your family). It may mean walking beside your spouse in a dark parking lot or holding each other close during a storm. Maybe it means protecting and shielding your spouse from negative aspects of yourself (such as mean words, irresponsible behaviors) by working hard to overcome those negatives. As you put treasuring into practice and focus on treating your spouse like a priceless gift, many of these negative aspects will disappear in your interactions with your spouse. All of these positive behaviors are protecting in nature and will help your spouse feel treasured.

U
Understanding your spouse's needs

Understanding is a fountain of life to those who have it.
—Proverbs 16:22

The differences between men and women are innumerable and evident in practically every area of our lives. It is no different when it comes to the needs each of us has in a marriage. What usually happens when we try to meet a need is that we give what we think *we* would need in that same situation. But due to our differences, this is usually the wrong thing. The Golden Rule of "Do unto others as you would have them do to you," should be looked at as a general concept. In general, how do you want your spouse to treat you? You want him or her to treasure you, to treat you with respect, to meet your needs. This is what you should do for him or her as well. However, if we take this verse and apply it to the *specific* things we can do for our spouses to help them feel those *general* concepts, we will likely miss the mark. Let's take an example.

Jim hardly ever gets sick, but when he does, it seems to slam him. A while back, he woke up in the middle of the night very ill. (I'll spare you the details.) By the time morning came, all he wanted to do was lie in bed and be left alone. I, of course, being the great wife that I am, knew that he needed much more than that. I was sure his road to health included the kids and me checking on him regularly, giving him hugs and kisses, and reminding him that we were here for him and loved him. We were often in his room asking if he needed anything or how we could make him more comfortable. After a couple of hours of that he became irritable (I guess he was allowed since he was sick) and in a less-than-pleasant tone of voice reminded me that all he wanted was some peace and quiet and to be left alone to sleep. I left with my tail between my legs, wondering how in the world that was going to make him feel better.

As you can probably guess, not long after this, it was my turn to be sick. (I know we are supposed to share everything, but this he could have kept to himself.) Jim left me alone in the bedroom to get some rest and did a wonderful job of keeping the children away. All too wonderful, actually. When I woke up, I realized that no one had checked on me in more than an hour. I wasn't getting any hugs and kisses or other special reminders that my family was around and ready to take care of me. They really were leaving me all alone. How in the world was that supposed to make me feel loved and cared for? I finally called for Jim and when he came, I asked him why he wasn't checking on me. His response was that he was working to keep the kids out of my hair so I could get some rest and start feeling better.

Even though both of us had good intentions and really wanted to meet the other's needs, we did not help by doing specifically what we ourselves would have needed in that situation. What we should have done instead was learn what the other needed and done that. The Golden Rule to apply to our specific behaviors in marriage goes more like this: Do Unto Others as They Need You to Do.

If you do not take time to find out specifically what your spouse needs, you are not likely to meet that need. Be sure to take time to share openly what you need from each other in different situations. Don't expect your spouse to read your mind.

Doing nice things for your spouse that do not meet his or her needs is like taking your car to get gas and holding the nozzle three feet away. You are expending energy (and money) as you let the gas pour out all over the pavement, and you only get a few drops in the car every now and then. The end result is that a lot more energy (and money) is put out than is received. When you give and give, but to areas that do not meet a need for your spouse, both of you end up feeling empty. Your spouse feels empty because he or she never got refueled. And you feel empty as well because you do not have an endless supply of energy to give. If you each take the time to really understand what the other needs, your efforts to fuel up by meeting each other's needs will be much more successful. And as you keep your spouse fueled up, he or she in turn will have the energy to give to you and therefore meet some of the specific needs you have. This is the give and take of a healthy relationship.

R
Romancing your spouse

My lover is mine, and I am his.
—Song of Songs 2:16

In this special team of marriage, the presence of romance definitely brings the couple closer together. Remember when you were dating and maybe in the early stages of marriage (before kids) when romance seemed to be everywhere? Whatever happened to that? It seems that, for most couples, the romance part of the relationship takes a nosedive shortly after marriage and then disappears even further once the kids start arriving. The focus moves away from wining and dining to eating and sleeping. You are confident that you have "caught" him or her and proven that you care. Then you slack off. How is your spouse to carry the feeling of being treasured from dating into marriage and then throughout the stages of marriage if you do not continue the behavior that made him or her feel treasured to begin with? And even if you were not a "Casanova" during dating, why not learn to be one now? Treasuring your spouse includes being romantic.

Romance involves proving that you think about your spouse when you are not together and showing your thoughtfulness when you are together. It involves taking time out of busy schedules to make each other feel loved, cared about, important, and special. It means taking the ordinary (dinner or a walk) and making it extraordinary (candlelit dinner or a walk in the moonlight). Through romantic gestures, you tell your spouse that he or she is the one and only one for you and worth the extra effort.

Never forget the importance of dating your spouse. This may seem elementary, but you may be surprised how many couples do not date anymore. Or if they do, it is only once or twice a year for special occasions. If you want your relationship to thrive and your spouse to feel treasured, spend quality couple time together. If possible, set aside a date night once a week. I have talked to many new (and not so new) parents who are wondering whether there will ever be time to date again. The time will be there as soon as you make it be there. Pencil it in to your schedule and do not let anything change it. I am sure both of you are missing those special times together, so stop letting the children eat up all of your time, and make time for a date!

I know that for some of you, the once-a-week date night may be difficult. But remember, you show that you treasure something by acting as though it is important to you. Spending time with your spouse shows that he or she is important to and treasured by you. You may need to change how you define "date" because of finances or time constraints. Don't get stuck in the rut of "dinner and a movie" dates. Get creative. Regardless of money and time excuses, you should never go more than one month without having a date. I recommend at least one date every week. As you get more creative, you may find yourselves having dates every few nights when you realize you do not even have to leave your house or spend any money.

E
Edifying your spouse

> Therefore encourage one another
> and build each other up.
> —1 Thessalonians 5:11

What do you see when you watch a team sporting event and someone on the team makes a great play? You see the rest of the team congratulating him, giving high fives, or slapping him on the rump in recognition of a job well done. They clap for each other, cheer each other on, and pour on the praise and compliments. Wouldn't that be a wonderful feeling to experience in your marriage?

To edify your spouse means to build him or her up, encourage, enhance self-esteem, and accept your spouse just as he or she is. You also edify by showing your appreciation for all your spouse does for you. Often the things our spouses do for us on a daily basis go unnoticed or unappreciated. The acts of kindness we receive, both large and small, if noticed at all, are often viewed as part of our spouse's job description. Even if we expect certain things, we should never forget to show appreciation for all they do for us. Take time every day to tell your spouse how much you appreciate him or her. Tell what you like about your spouse. It is always nice to hear what someone else likes about us. It reinforces healthy self-esteem.

It is so easy when you are tired and stressed and generally worn out to become negative and critical. You may begin to notice only when something goes wrong, and the words out of your mouth may become more discouraging than encouraging. For a marriage and a family to grow stronger, you need to encourage each other. Learn to focus more on the positives than the negatives. Work to catch your spouse (and your children) being good, and remember to tell them how much they mean to you.

Pulling It All Together

Treasuring your spouse may feel like an overwhelming task. But it really does not have to be hard work. Nurturing a marriage is much like growing a garden. Once you have cultivated and prepared the ground through the dating stage and planted the seed at the wedding, you have done most of the hard work. From there, what is really required to keep your marriage garden growing is just some daily attention. If you will take some time every day to participate in one or more of the parts of TREASURE, you will be giving your relationship the nourishment it needs to continue growing into the beautiful garden God intended it to be.

Coming Up Next ...

To continue making your marriage stronger, give it some of your time. Can you imagine planting a garden and then walking away and not putting any more time into it? What would you expect to see when you came back? The longer you neglect your marriage and do not spend time nourishing it, the worse the garden will look. The next chapter will help you learn the essential element of spending time together as a couple and will give you suggestions as to how to find this priceless treasure even through the parenting years.

CHAPTER FIVE

TIME FOR A
TIME-OUT

Essential Element 5: Time Together

You are watching your favorite team play the big game. They have moved down the field well and are now sitting within scoring distance of the goal. The anticipation and the pressure are building, and the play is just about to begin. And then you hear a whistle blow and see the signal indicating that a time-out has been called.

In most sports, a time-out is a break from the action of the game. It is a valuable time for the members of the team to regroup, reevaluate, and check in with each other about how the game is going, what adjustments they need to make, and what's coming up next. This private team time allows the players to make sure everyone understands the plays.

When you think about it, isn't that just exactly what many of our marriages need during the parenting season? We need to take a break from the action of this "game." We need to take some time to slow down and get away from the constant pressure of parenting, time to regroup and check in with our teammates. Parents need private time to continue to feel as though they are not only parents but also partners. This is an essential element to keeping your team on track.

Finding a Balance

How do you know if you and your spouse are not spending enough time together? Is it possible to spend too much time together? What if each of you has different views regarding the amount of time you need together? These questions are important to consider as you work on finding a balance in the amount of time you spend with each other, alone, with children, at work, and any other activity that requires your time.

We all understand that for a marriage to grow we need to give it some attention. That is hard to do if we do not spend any time together. Spending time together seemed to come easy (or at least easier) when we were dating and even in the early years of marriage. Why is it so hard now? In part it has to do with having more responsibilities, such as children who take up a good portion of our lives. But when you really think about it, you had responsibilities earlier in your life together, too. The difference really has more to do with effort and importance of the activity than it does with responsibilities. But finding the right balance of time with your spouse can be difficult.

How do you know if you and your spouse are not spending enough time together? Perhaps you start to feel distant. One of you may make comments such as, "I've really been missing you lately," "We just never seem to find time for each other any more," or, "I'm feeling really lonely." Take statements like this seriously and discuss them. When you are spending too little time together as a couple, the two of you will start to grow apart and begin feeling distant and neglected. You may notice tension growing if you continue to neglect quality time together. The tension grows out of a lack of attention. All of us need attention, and if we are not receiving positive attention and quality time together, we will likely seek out negative attention. Even negative attention (arguments) is better than no attention at all.

To remedy this problem, set a time to talk about your personal needs and share how much time you feel you need to spend together in order to feel connected and close. Then start working to make it a priority to make that time to be together. Make sure you give each other as much positive attention as you possibly can. As you discuss these issues, pay close attention to see whether one of you experiences a feeling of love particularly through the spending of time together. This may be your "love language," and therefore it must be learned and spoken in your home.

Now let's look at the other extreme. Is it possible for a couple to spend too much time together? Believe it or not, yes! Spending too much time together can cause you to become isolated from friends and the rest of the world and to become too dependent on each other. Too much time together can also lead to an increase in tension and arguments between you.

Jim and I found out fairly early in our relationship that we can spend too much time together. We had been married two years and were planning our first "real" vacation together. We had gone on some weekend getaways, but this was going to be a full seven days in Mexico. We couldn't wait. Life had been hectic over the previous couple of years with me in graduate school and Jim working long hours to support us, so the idea of a whole week of uninterrupted time together seemed like heaven. And it was—for the first four days. We had a wonderful time sitting on the beach, sightseeing, and really having the time to talk and catch up with each other. Then day five arrived with a bang.

I do not remember what started the whole thing, but before we even made it to breakfast we were being snippy with each other. By noon, it had become a full-blown argument about heaven knows what and we definitely were not enjoying this time together. Eventually, Jim realized this was going nowhere and decided that we just needed a break from each other for a few hours. By that time, I thoroughly agreed, and we went our own ways. Jim headed for the golf course with a new friend. And I headed for the beach with a good book. Although it took me a little while to calm down and start enjoying my solitude, once I did, I realized this was just what I needed—some time to myself on the beach just reading and relaxing. We had been spending time on the beach on the other days, but Jim is not much for just sitting and reading. He likes to be up doing something. So when we were relaxing I would be worrying that he was getting bored. But this day was all mine, and I was loving it.

By the time Jim returned from his golf game, he, too, was in a much brighter mood. We were able to reconnect and apologize for the early morning tactics. We both decided there were better ways to get some alone time than causing a fight, and we committed to simply ask for it in the future. Today, if we take an extended vacation, we try to plan in some self time on about day four to avoid a repeat of the Mexico encounter, and it seems to work.

Different personalities have different needs for alone time and couple time. It will be important for you both to identify what your specific needs are. Take time to talk openly about how much time you need together in order to feel treasured. Also share how much individual time you are comfortable with. As you do this, begin working on reaching a compromise that will meet the needs of both of you.

Evaluating Your Need for Time Together

Now that you understand that each of you may have different needs in regard to the amount of time you spend together, it is time to get together and discuss this. The best way to start moving toward scheduling the right amount of time together is to just sit down and discuss the following points:

1. How much time do each of you need together to feel valued by the other?
2. What is realistic to expect?
3. What might need to be adjusted to allow more couple time?
4. What are some ideas of how you would spend the time together?
5. How do each of you define "fun"?
6. How will you share making the arrangements for your time together?
7. What personal considerations need to be taken into account (work schedules, morning vs. evening person, likes and dislikes)?
8. How soon can you get started? Set the date and keep it. Then set the next date before the first one ends, or consider making a set schedule for these encounters.

Making Time Together a Priority

We all are aware of the lack of time we seem to have these days. As our society and the world seem to move faster and faster, we become caught up in the rapids and are pushed downstream so fast that it makes our heads spin. We may feel as though we are drowning in a sea of responsibilities and commitments that seldom allows us to come up for air. If we do not make the effort to get out of this mess, our marriages and our families may be destroyed. But there is hope. If you can commit to reaching the shore and pulling yourself out of the water, you will have a new vantage point from which to make some healthier decisions. No one is going to push you back in, but if you stand too close, you may find yourself being pulled back into the myriad activities and responsibilities that can drown your relationships.

As you step back from your daily life and take an honest look at all the things that fill your time and overwhelm you, what do you see? Is every spare second filled with something to do or somewhere to go? Who and what are taking up the majority of your time, energy, and resources? As you begin to consider all that you do, are you pleased with what you see? Are you spending the most time with the things that are genuinely most important to you? If not, why not?

These may be difficult and painful questions to ask yourself, but they are necessary if you are going to learn to keep the people who are most important to you as your top priority. Take a minute to evaluate your past couple of weeks. Based on what you see, would you say you are working harder to be "Superparent" or "Superspouse"? Have you put your spouse on the back burner repetitively, evaluating that what your child needs is more important? When was the last time you made sure your spouse knew that he or she was number one with you?

If you are always pushing your spouse aside for time with the kids, you may want to consider just what you are teaching your children. By the way you treat your spouse, are you modeling for your children how you hope they will treat their future spouses? Probably not. Spending time with your spouse not only draws the two of you closer together, but it also teaches your children that the marital relationship has to be our number one human relationship.

One of the major components of strengthening your marital team is to make sure you spend adequate time together. Now, I know that many of you already are coming up with a list of excuses as to why you cannot find the time to spend with each other. I'm here to tell you—you can. Healthy couples do not "find" the time to be together, they "make" time to be together. You may have convinced yourself that you simply do not have enough time to schedule each other into your day, but this is not accurate. You have the time to do whatever you want to do. And if you do not spend the time with your spouse, you will simply fill the time with something less important.

Budgeting Your Time

Setting priorities is much like financial budgeting. You understand that you have a limited supply of money and that your money is going to get spent somewhere. Taking time to budget your money means that you actively choose where to spend your money. You know that if you do not do this, you will likely spend little bits of money here and there, and then when it comes time to pay the big bills, you will not have enough left.

The same principle applies to time. You know that you have only twenty-four hours in a day and that your time is going to be spent doing something. You can either actively choose where you spend your time or not; it is up to you. But if you do not budget your time, you may find your day, week, or month eaten away by trivial and less-important things. Then, when you need to spend time with someone or something really important to you, there will not be any time left. Budgeting time and setting priorities help you make sure that you get the biggest and most important things done first. Let me share an illustration that I sometimes use when I speak on priorities.

I take out a large glass mason jar that represents our lives. We have only so much space and time to fill. I start to fill the jar with some rocks from my yard. These rocks represent the "big" important things in our lives. I work and maneuver them around until I can fit in as many as possible, which is usually about five or six. Then I ask the audience if the container is full. Most will say yes, but I can always tell where the moms are in the audience because they seem to be the ones saying no. And they are right. It is not full. I prove this by pouring some small pea-sized gravel into the jar.

I ask again if it is full. This gets a more mixed response from the audience, who is now beginning to see where I'm going with this. I assure them again that the jar is still not full as I pour sand into the jar. As the sand begins to move into all the little spaces left by the bigger rocks, the jar is finally beginning to look really full. When I ask the audience if the jar is full, I hear a solid yes (even from the mothers this time). But one final time, I inform them that it is not, and I pull out a pitcher of water and pour it in.

What is the purpose of this illustration? To explain that if we are careful to fit the biggest and most important things into our lives first, we will find that there is still room for much more. However, if we first fill our lives with all the little things (i.e., if I had started by putting in the water, sand, and gravel), then when it is time to make room for the big things, there is no way to fit them all in.

I hope that as you work through this chapter, you will understand the importance of making time to be together with your sweetheart. It will also be important for the two of you to work together to set the priorities for your family, or you may find yourselves going in different directions and being at odds with each other.

Each of us individually will develop a set of priorities that we use (either consciously or unconsciously) to manage our time and resources. These priorities are what help us make both large and small decisions in daily life. But when developed individually, they will likely conflict with the priorities of our spouses. This will make sense only when you realize and admit that most of us are beings who like to have things our own way, at least most of the time. When your private priorities are not openly identified and discussed with your spouse, conflict will surely result at some point.

He wants to play golf on his one and only day off; she hopes for a break from the kids.

She wants to get the house cleaned; he is focused on washing the cars.

He works overtime to make extra money to pay off some bills; she wants him home in the evening for a family meal.

She wants to put the tax-return money in the savings account for a rainy day; he wants to go on a family vacation.

See how easily our different priorities can show up and likely cause conflict in the home? The issue is not usually the right vs. wrong of the priorities, but rather the compatibility of them. Learning to identify each of your individual priorities is the first step in developing a mutually satisfying set of priorities that will serve your whole family.

Building the Priority Ladder

I like to look at priorities as rungs on a very tall ladder. Everything in our lives occupies one rung of the ladder, with the top rungs being the most important or pressing at the moment, and the lower rungs being less pressing. For example, at this very moment, the number one rung for me is writing this section about priorities (number one for you would be reading it). But my ladder does not have only one rung. Taking my kids to their gymnastics class might be about rung number six, looking for a new house about number twelve, and cleaning out the closet somewhere around 187. Everything fits somewhere, and eventually everything gets a chance to occupy the number one spot. (When I finally get around to cleaning out that closet sometime next century, it will be number one for at least a moment or two.)

Some things in our lives tend to occupy that coveted number one spot on a fairly regular basis, and these are the things we need to identify and evaluate. Those things in your life that occupy the top five rungs of your priority ladder are the ones that easily alternate into the number one position and are therefore the most valued by you. One way to evaluate your top five is to look through your checkbook and your planner. Where we spend our time and our money will often tell us what we value. Some of the things you may find in your top five might include job, school, children, religion, recreation, spouse, self, cleaning, friends, hobbies, and so forth. As you identify your priorities, remember that the top five are all fairly equal in their importance to you. In other words, at any given moment, depending on the circumstances, any of these five could take over the number one position.

Let me give you an example using my own top five list. The top five rungs of my priority ladder include, in no particular order: my job, my children, my marriage/spouse, myself, and my relationship with Jesus. Now, let's say I am at work, in the middle of a session, and I get buzzed. The school just called to say Taffeta has fallen on the playground and is hurt. My number one rung, which was occupied by my job, immediately gets replaced. My child becomes number one as I leave the session to go care for her. Or maybe I am on a date with Jim, and the pager goes off. Again, number one changes quickly, as I move from my spouse to my job this time. And here is a no-brainer: I am actually in the middle of cleaning out that closet that has needed it for the past century when I get a call from a friend inviting me to a movie with the girls. That number 187 that had finally made it to the number one is quickly forgotten, and self time jumps into number one spot.

Evaluating Your Priorities

Take a few minutes right now to identify what you believe to be your top five priorities. Grab a piece of paper and write down what you believe you are spending the majority of your time, energy, and money on. This is not the time to write down the "right" answer (we all know what *should* be there). This is a time to get very honest with yourself. Where do you really spend most of your time, energy, and money? What do your behaviors identify as being most valuable to you? What might I say your priorities are, based on observing your life for a week or two?

Now that you have identified your top five priorities, it is time to evaluate them. Is there anything that surprises you? Or, more important, is there anything *not* on your list that should be? One of the most important things for you as a married person is to make sure that both your spouse and you are present in the top five. It is not only healthy but also necessary that both you and your spouse rank high on each of your lists. Have you ever considered what can happen if both of you are not on the other's top five rungs?

Putting yourself on one of the top five rungs on the ladder and not putting your spouse there means trouble. You are being selfish and focused on what you want. You are not acting as part of the marital team. You are hot-dogging it and grabbing the ball and keeping it for as long as you can to satisfy your own desires, no matter the fallout. Or maybe you see that you haven't put either your spouse or yourself on the top five. That would indicate that most likely your children and their activities are eating up more than their fair share of the top spots.

On the other hand, putting your spouse and children but not yourself in your top five is also unhealthy and can damage the relationship in the long run. Don't get me wrong; those around you will love it and think you are great for always putting them first. But over time, you will find that you have been doing all the giving and not getting anything (or very little) in return. Eventually, the well runs dry and you will have nothing left to give. Anger has built up, and you find yourself feeling resentful about the giving that you once enjoyed.

So go back now and look at your top five list. If you see that neither your spouse nor you are there, continue filling in the rungs of your priority ladder until both of you are on the list. How far did you have to go? What does this tell you about changes you need to make?

Now take a minute to do this same exercise for your spouse. What do you see as the major priorities in his or her life? Once both you and your spouse have done this exercise, find some time alone as a couple to discuss your lists. Ask your spouse to share with you his or her top five. Carefully and lovingly discuss changes that you each need to make to bring your priorities into line.

As we end this chapter, I want to remind you that happy, healthy couples do not "find" time to be together; they "make" time to be together. Start making time for each other right now. Make it your number one priority to make sure your spouse knows and feels that he or she is number one to you. Here is a list of suggestions for creating quality couple time together to help get you started.

Creating Quality Time Together

1. Have a date away from the house. Hire a sitter and get out for a real, old-fashioned date. Try to have a date night at least once a week.

2. Learn to date at home. Creating special time at home for just the two of you can fill the spot of a date when you cannot get a sitter or afford to go out.

3. Avoid overcommitting. Be selective about what outside events and responsibilities you commit to. Be sure to check with your spouse before committing.

4. Set aside daily "mommy-and-daddy" time. Even fifteen to twenty minutes a day can help you continue to feel connected. Taking this time daily helps your children learn to respect your couple time and models to them how important you are to each other.

5. Become interested in what your spouse is interested in so you can start doing it together. When I started taking an interest in football, Jim was thrilled. Now we hardly ever miss a

game, and I am often the one who wants to rush home after church to catch the game.

6. Read the newspaper together. Share your thoughts and feelings about what is going on in the world.

7. Share a cup of coffee together before the kids wake up or some other beverage after they go to bed.

8. Go on a walk together. Consider having the older kids watch the younger ones, and take a walkie-talkie or cell phone with you in case of emergency.

9. Put a lock on your bedroom door—and use it.

10. Send the kids to bed early. They need more rest than you may realize, and you need the quality time together.

Coming Up Next ...

Of all the essential elements presented in this book, the next one is the greatest. Whether or not you are able to communicate with each other is the make-it-or-break-it element of building a strong marriage–parenting team. No matter how skilled you are at the other elements, not being able to communicate can destroy a marriage. So, if you are ready to really focus on your team's most essential secret weapon for success, turn the page and let the training begin.

CHAPTER SIX

CAN WE TALK ABOUT IT?

Essential Element 6: Communication

*I*f there is one essential element on which all the others rest, it would be this one—the ability to communicate. No matter how good a team is at all the other skills, none of them really matter if the team members do not communicate. It is much like what Scripture tells us about how important the ability to love is to our Christian walk. In 1 Corinthians chapter 13, Paul explained that nothing we do means anything if we do not have love. Love is the most essential element of our spiritual journey. And communication is the most essential element to marriage. Within a marriage, if you do not have good communication skills, you have nothing. Just about anything can be worked out if a couple can just talk about it. Unfortunately, however, many couples have never developed the skills of healthy communication and conflict resolution. The absence of these skills is most evident when the storms of life hit—and parenting is one of the most furious. Without good communication skills, the couple will either struggle enormously as they try to survive the storm, or they may simply give up when the pressures of parenting hit. This chapter will focus on the two core elements in the ability to communicate: listening and talking. Then we will discuss the art of conflict resolution in the next chapter.

Communicating Is Important

Communication is essential for any team, not only during the game but before and after as well. Teams spend time making sure they understand each other, use the same playbook, and have the same plans and strategies for the game. Communication is essential to pull off those plays and keep the players moving toward their common goal of adjusting to new situations. After the game, they learn from successes and mistakes.

If you hope to win the prize of a marriage that lasts for a lifetime in the game of life, communication is a must. You need to be able to discuss and understand each other's differences in how you interpret certain words or situations if you want to be able to avoid some conflicts. You need not only to feel that you are being listened to and really heard, but you also need the freedom to talk and share at a deep, intimate level in an emotionally safe environment.

ECHO-ing Is Effective Listening

ECHO conversation combines all the necessary elements of listening in a way that your spouse will know for sure that you have understood what he or she was trying to say. ECHO-ing involves the process of actively focusing your attention on what your spouse is saying, including both verbal and nonverbal information—and then reflecting—or "echoing," to your spouse what you heard. At some time in your life, you have probably stood at the bottom of a canyon and bellowed out a greeting, hoping to hear your words bounce back to you. People of all ages will yell out ridiculous phrases and wait for the echo. But can you imagine the looks on their faces if they yelled out, "I love you," and a moment later the canyon echoed, "Who cares," or, "Yeah, sure you do"? Yet, in our marriages, conversations can often become that distorted. Using ECHO conversation will help you hear what your spouse is really trying to say.

How It Works

ECHO conversation has four basic parts:
E: Establish and explain
C: Concentrate
H: Highlight the main points
O: Obtain agreement and understanding

E
Establish and explain

To begin an ECHO conversation, one of you will need to define the issue you need to discuss and then pick a time to sit down and talk. ("Honey, I really need to talk to you about our plans for summer vacation. Could we make some time around eight o'clock tonight?") As you do this, one of you is the speaker and the other, of course, is the listener. The speaker's job is to explain his or her thoughts and feelings about the established topic. Remember that your spouse is trying to listen and preparing to echo. If you go off on a ten-minute tirade, most of what you say will get lost. Be concise and to the point.

C
Concentrate

As the speaker is talking, the listener's job is to *listen!* This means you must stop talking and concentrate on what the person is saying, as well as on how it is being said. Focus your attention on the words and ideas. But be sure not to miss the attitudes and feelings also being expressed through body language, tone of voice, gestures, and facial expressions. These nonverbal aspects of communication often will give you an accurate indication of the speaker's attitude and emotional state, regardless of the words.

Be careful not to interrupt either verbally or mentally. Interrupting is probably the most destructive element to communication. If you give the speaker time to say what he or she has to say, you may find that your questions will be addressed. But even if you are not verbally interrupting, you may be mentally interrupting. Mental interruptions include arguing in your head or jumping to conclusions and assuming you know what your spouse is going to say next. When you do this, you tune out the rest of what the speaker says. You are deciding what your comeback is going to be or maybe just arguing within yourself: "I can't believe she just said that!" You may be thinking, "Hurry up and finish; I've got your point," or, "Yes, yes, I know what you mean." Not only does this show disrespect, but also you just might be wrong in your conclusions. Waiting and listening will keep you from putting your foot in your mouth or from starting an argument. Even more important, it shows that you value what your spouse is saying as more important than what you want to say.

Avoid outside distractions. The television, telephone, dinner preparation, and children all fit into this category. It is practically impossible to concentrate on what the speaker is saying with only part of your brain working on it. To really listen, you need to totally focus your attention. Choose the right time to hold an important conversation. Don't attempt it right before your spouse's favorite television program or if you are expecting an important call or preparing dinner. Parents of young children seem to be especially affected in this area. It seems inevitable that children *need* to talk to us the minute we attempt to hold an adult conversation. Many mothers actually become quite good at hearing and even responding to multiple conversations simultaneously. Responding is not listening. If you choose to talk about serious matters during these times, you are flirting with disaster. Avoid times that you know will be packed with distractions.

There is also nothing wrong with teaching your children to "wait just a minute." Learning not to interrupt others will serve them well in the future. But please remember that a child's definition of "minute" may be quite different from yours. So as your children learn to wait, don't put them off too long or they will begin to feel ignored.

H
Highlight the main points

When your spouse has finished speaking, take a moment to consider what you have heard, then echo it. Your words may not be exactly the words your spouse spoke. The echo should reflect the main points along with any emotional undertones that may have changed the meaning of the words you heard. You will be summarizing what you heard by adding in all the cues you were aware of and the main points presented. It is important to remember here that this is not the place or time for you to add your own thoughts, opinions, judgments, or rebuttals. Just focus on what the speaker said.

Let's say the speaker is sitting with arms and legs crossed and turned away from you. With an angry scowl and in a rough voice your spouse says, "No! I'm not angry!" You could respond, "What I heard you say is that you are not angry. Is that what you meant to say?" But if that were your response, you would not have been using the ECHO conversation skills. You would just have been hearing. The ECHO response would have been, "What I heard you say is that you are angry, but you don't want to talk about it right now. Is that what you meant to say?" See the difference? ECHO-ing takes into account all you are seeing, hearing, and sensing in order to come to a conclusion.

Notice in the example that the listener used two phrases the speaker did not. The first is, "What I *heard* you say was...." This is different from, "What you said was...." The latter implies that the listener will be right. And if the speaker does not agree that the echo was an accurate representation of what was meant, the implication is that he or she must be wrong. This can quickly lead to defensiveness and an argument about who said what or who is right. A simple change in words can avoid this. "What I *heard* you say was ..." allows room for either party to change or disagree without the "right or wrong" issue coming up.

The second key phrase, "Is that what you *meant* to say?" should be the final phrase the listener says. If you say, "Is that what you said?" and the speaker says, "No, that's not what I said," then the right and wrong issue rears its head again. This time, however, it looks as though the listener is the one who is wrong. Asking, "Is that what you *meant* to say?" allows the speaker to hear how he or she came across to the listener. Then the speaker can adjust what he or she was trying to convey without either person becoming defensive.

O
Obtain agreement and understanding

The final step in ECHO conversation involves the listener obtaining agreement from the speaker that the listener has completely heard and understood what the speaker was trying to say. You must reach this agreement before giving the listener a turn to discuss the established topic. Once the listener asks, "Is that what you meant to say?" then the speaker needs to respond either yes or no: yes if the listener did get the main points, no if the listener missed something or if the speaker wants to adjust what he or she was trying to say. The speaker will say the things he or she wants to add or change, or things that were not understood. Continue this process until the speaker feels he or she has been completely heard. You will know you have reached agreement when the listener asks "Is that what you meant to say?" and speaker responds with, "Yes!"

Both Have a Chance to Speak

At times, ECHO conversation may end at this point. There may be conversations that involve only one spouse needing to share about something personal. In those cases, the ECHO-ing is complete when that speaker feels completely heard and understood. However, many marital conversations involve both of you; you want to be sure that both parties have the chance to express themselves and be understood. When this is the case, the two of you simply take turns being speaker and listener. The first speaker stays in that role until you complete all four steps of ECHO-ing. Then the second speaker can address the original issue as if he or she had been the *first* one to speak. Share your original thoughts and feelings about the topic, instead of responding to what the other person just said.

Once both of you have had a chance to share your thoughts and feelings, and have really felt heard, then you can begin to respond to each other's thoughts. At this stage, the more natural back-and-forth conversation can occur. But if at any point during the discussion either of you does not feel heard or feels things could be going in a negative direction, simply start ECHO-ing again.

Now that you have a clear understanding of the importance of listening, let's turn our attention to the other main part of communication—talking.

Talking Builds Intimacy

Talking to each other is one of the strongest ways to build intimacy and closeness, and therefore one of the most important aspects of any relationship, especially marriage. One reason we tend to communicate better and more during dating is because we are focused on *building* intimacy and closeness. Once we feel the relationship is established, we stop focusing on building it and too often believe it to be a "finished project" in need of little or no attention. A relationship is never a finished project. A relationship is ever growing and ever changing and will require constant attention and maintenance to stay healthy and in good repair.

Not all talking will lead to greater intimacy and closeness. Talking about who won the playoff game last night, what the weather is supposed to be next week, or the great deal you got at the sidewalk sale today is not going to bring those benefits. Just talking, regardless of the topic, will not grow intimacy. We score true intimacy only when we reach deep into ourselves and are willing to risk sharing from our hearts. However, most conversations should at least be building blocks for developing more intimacy between the two of you. Scoring intimacy does not come without its fair share of effort, teamwork, and risk-taking. Let's look at the different levels of risk in communications you must endure to win intimacy.

Communication Progresses through Five Levels

What you talk about will make the difference in your feelings of closeness in a relationship. If talking about just anything developed intimacy, then we all would likely go around feeling intimate with our co-workers, grocery clerks, mail carriers, and bill collectors. We know this is not the case. Depending on the relationship you have with the person you are talking to, you may share at any one of five levels of communication as defined by John Powell in his book, *Why Am I Afraid to Tell You Who I Am?*[1] Let's take time to understand these levels and determine at what level the benefits of closeness and intimacy actually develop. The following explanation of these levels is loosely adapted from Powell's definitions.

PreGame Show: Level 1. It's game day. You have the television on, but the game has not started. Pregame is a part of game day, but it is not what you look forward to. What people are saying does not really matter. You only half listen as you walk through the room doing other things. Overall, you do not have much interest in all this chatter. You know it is impossible for your team to score before the game has even started. So you just go about preparing your hot wings, refilling your plate, or running to the bathroom and waiting for the real action to start.

This level of communication is superficial and involves no personal sharing. At this level, we often ask questions that we do not really care if we get an answer to, do not care what the answer is, or already know what the answer is supposed to be. These interactions are brief and often viewed only as a social obligation, not as a desire to really get to know the other person: "How are you?"; "Where did you get that hat?"; or "Did you enjoy the movie?"

Coin Toss: Level 2. The food is prepared, the guests have arrived, and the game is about to begin. The room has not quieted down, but everyone is aware that something is beginning. Although the coin toss is necessary, it is not a make-or-break part of the game. It does signify that the game is beginning and is of some interest. But it is not something that involves any skill, personal involvement, or risk on the part of the teams.

Conversation at this level is slightly deeper than the first level. It involves sharing some basic information that you feel will be of interest to someone. You talk about other people and what they may have said or done. You merely report the facts, much like the six o'clock news. You do not enhance the facts by presenting personal opinion. You do not take any personal risk because the information is not about you: "Did you hear about Bob and Mary? They're having some marital problems"; "There was an accident on the expressway that had traffic backed up for five miles."

First and Ten, Do It Again: Level 3. Now this is really part of the game. The players are on the field, the whistle has been blown, and the action has started. Now people are paying more attention to the television and talking less, although there is still room to move around without feeling as though you have missed much. Your team's ability to reach first-down status over and over again is important. These first downs move your team down the field and into scoring position. You know there is a risk taken on every play, but risks are necessary if you are going to win this game.

This is the first level of *real* communication. At this level, we begin to take risks. We may present information and then add personal thoughts. We also may simply present our opinions, judgments, and decisions on their own. Either way, at this level we are sharing cautiously, and we will retreat quickly if we feel that what we are saying is not accepted. This is the "I think …" level, where we share what is in our heads or minds. We may debate our positions, but only from a logical point of view, continuing to keep our feelings far from view: "I think all restaurants should be smoke-free"; "I'm considering getting a part-time job to help out with the finances."

Inside the Red Zone: Level 4. Things are really heating up. Your team has moved down the field and has made it inside the other team's twenty-yard line. The intensity and anticipation of a score is all that anyone can feel. Your team is more vulnerable as the other team also turns up the heat and feels threatened. You know your team has a couple of chances for a big score here. Even if that doesn't materialize, you will at least score some points through a field goal. Your team calls a time-out and heads to the sidelines for a huddle.

At this level of communication, we reach the point of true risk-taking. This is the "I feel …" level, where we open up and share from our hearts and express our feelings and emotions. We may still present information from the earlier levels of facts and our ideas or judgments about those facts, but we go one step deeper and also share the feelings underneath the thoughts. If true intimacy is going to develop between two people, they must both reach the point of opening up and sharing from their feelings: "I was really scared when I heard you had a wreck"; "I love my children, but sometimes I feel I am going crazy when I've been with them all day. I just need a break."

"TOUCHDOWN!" Level 5. All eyes are on the television, and the room is silent as the play begins. This is definitely a make-or-break play. The risks are great, but the potential for scoring makes it all worth it. The ball is snapped and then in the air for what seems like eternity. As everything seems to move in slow motion, you wonder whether the receiver will be in position to make the catch or if the chance to score will be ripped away. You have watched this team work well together for years, and that calms you down. This is the kind of play they have been practicing for, and they are ready. As the ball is caught, the crowd and the team erupt in cheers. TOUCH-DOWN!

At this level of completely open, truthful communication, true intimacy is reached. Although this level definitely presents the greatest level of risk, it also presents the greatest potential for scoring intimacy. As we risk rejection by being vulnerable and allowing others to see us as we really are, we also allow the potential for others to accept us unconditionally and without reservation. We are able to move beyond statements such as, "If he really knew me, he wouldn't like me" to statements like, "Because she really knows me, she can accept me as I am"; "I'm really afraid I won't be a good mom because I never had a mom to show me what to do"; "Please don't leave the room when we are discussing something. That always reminds me of my dad walking out on my mom."

It Is Time to Evaluate

Now that we have looked at the five levels of communication we are most likely to use in our relationships, it is time for you to evaluate at which level you tend to spend most of your time. Throughout any given day, you likely communicate to some extent at each of these levels with those people around you, even your spouse. Don't assume that you must always score a touchdown by communicating at level 5 in order to have a thriving marriage. That would be impossible for anyone to sustain. Level 5 communication takes time and energy that may not always be available. Besides, how deep can a conversation be about who is supposed to take Johnny to soccer practice Monday night or whether to have chicken or spaghetti for dinner? There definitely is an appropriate place within a marital relationship for conversations that remain at levels 2 and 3. However, within a marriage, level 1 communication should be minimal. We should not be interacting with our spouses simply out of social grace or obligation, and we should always be interested in what their responses will be to our questions. If, through your personal evaluation, you realize that you and your spouse practically never communicate at a level 5 but tend to stay at the safer levels, such as levels 1 to 3, then your marriage likely is suffering. It will be important for both of you to begin risking again and sharing feelings that you have kept inside. You may need to relearn some skills to create a safe environment for sharing. Appendix B, "How to Nourish a Conversation," presents several suggestions that will help get you back on the right track. If you have avoided honest sharing for an extended period, you may need to seek professional help to begin opening up again and taking risks to restore intimacy.

Coming Up Next ...

Strong communication skills such as listening and talking are essential parts of a healthy marriage. We need these skills because every relationship will experience storms in the form of conflicts, disagreements, negative emotions, or flat-out fights. It is not the presence or absence of these storms that is most important. Rather, it is a couple's ability to weather these storms that makes the difference between a winning team and a losing team. Couples who have learned to manage conflict in a healthy manner are happier and more stable than those who have not learned this skill. In chapter 7 you will learn how to be one of those couples who can weather the storms of conflict.

CHAPTER SEVEN

AVOID GETTING THROWN OUT OF THE GAME

Essential Element 7: FAIR Fighting

*W*hen tensions run high and the pressure is on in the big game, tempers may flare. At some point during the game, a coach or player may disagree with a referee's call. There are appropriate ways to express that disagreement. However, if the offended coach or player loses control of his or her temper, you are likely to hear, "You're outta here!" And that person's participation in that game is over.

Conflicts and disagreements are a given in both sports and marriage. It is not the presence of these that should concern us but rather our ability to resolve them by using the rules of fair play. By agreeing to a particular set of rules of conduct and following them, the members of a team are assured that conflicts can be resolved in a healthy manner.

Why a Whole Chapter on Fighting?

It has been said that "marriage is the only game that both people can win."[1] I would add, "or that both can lose." I would define "winning" as having a growing relationship that provides intimacy and satisfaction and lasts for a lifetime. Based on this definition, both parties either win or lose. Although some relationships may last for a lifetime, they are not all described as satisfactory or intimate by the parties involved. Several researchers have studied long-standing relationships to try to identify what separates the satisfied from the dissatisfied couples. One major answer tends to surface every time—constructive problem-solving, or conflict-resolution skills.[2]

Let's get real here. All of us are going to have disagreements. We are humans, and each of us is different from the next one. We have different personalities, opinions, and feelings. Most of us like to express our personal thoughts and opinions to those closest to us. Since it is impossible that you are exactly like your spouse, then it is also impossible to completely avoid disagreements. Research has shown that couples who are able to successfully resolve differences when they develop have the best chance to go on to have a long-term, successful marriage.[3]

In other words, happy couples have developed various healthy ways of handling the inevitable conflicts. Unhappy couples probably have not. If the goal of this book is to help you develop the strongest relationship team possible, then it would make sense to spend at least some time teaching the essential skill of resolving conflicts. The win–win result comes when a marriage–parent team is able to resolve a disagreement together and thus create a deeper understanding and respect between themselves. This will also protect the parental team from children's attempts to drive a wedge between the two of you, because you are working together as a team.

We will first take some time to describe what many couples are doing wrong in conflict resolution. Then I will present one technique you can use to start fighting FAIR and will give you some specific rules to follow.

Is Anger Wrong?

Isn't it wrong to be angry with my spouse? Absolutely not! Anger is simply a feeling. Feelings are neither right nor wrong; they are just feelings. And unless you are a robot or other inanimate object, you cannot avoid feeling anger at some point in your relationship. Some of us experience it more often than others, but the experience of anger in a relationship is not wrong. The Bible addresses the emotion of anger specifically, and nowhere does it say, "Do not feel angry." In Psalm 4:4 and again in Ephesians 4:26, Scripture says, "In your anger, do not sin." The assumption is that you will feel anger, and when you do, you are called not to sin. Feeling angry does not mean that you do not love each other. It does not mean that either of you is bad. It only means that you are human. By believing that it is *wrong* to feel angry within a marriage, you would set an unrealistic expectation for you and your spouse and would likely doom your relationship to failure.

Conflict is a part of any relationship and is often the result of the natural differences between two people or of unmet needs within the relationship. Anger can be a warning sign that something is wrong or that conflicts are not being resolved. It may signal that if something does not change, damage may result.

I sometimes think of anger as being like the tornado siren in our neighborhood. Its blaring is often unexpected and can sound very loud, depending on how close you are to it. It signals imminent danger. Although it can evoke feelings of fear, anxiety, or even panic, it almost always causes us to take action. We become aware of potential destruction that could be right around the corner and are moved to evaluate the situation. We take this warning seriously and immediately do what we can to avoid harm to ourselves and our loved ones.

None of us would view the tornado siren as "wrong." Even though it may make us uncomfortable, we are thankful it is there to help us avoid future harm. We also should not view the anger in a relationship as wrong. Instead, we can view anger as a sign that something is posing a danger to our relationship. Anger is a signal that something needs to change. Then we can move to correct and resolve the problem as soon as possible.

What Are We Doing Wrong?

If you are one of those unhappy couples who has not learned to resolve conflict, you may want to evaluate how you and your spouse handle your disagreements. Professor Howard Markman has done extensive research on the impact of conflict on the marital relationship. The following is an overview of Professor Markman's four specific patterns of conflictual interactions that often lead to marital problems.[4] As you read through these, evaluate which, if any, you are practicing in your marriage.

1. Escalation. This is the "one-up" style of conflict. It occurs when the argument becomes focused on responding back and forth to each other in a progressively more negative manner. It may start with something fairly trivial, but soon the mudslinging and verbal abuse cause the feelings of anger and frustration to peak. This is a destructive pattern of interacting because, as the disagreement continues to escalate, partners will eventually say something that strikes the very core of hurt and pain in the other. And although the things we say out of anger often do not reflect our real feelings, the damage is done. Once we have said certain things, they are difficult to forget. We damage long-term intimacy if, at a more intimate moment, we use statements as weapons to hurt each other. This will make future attempts at communication even more difficult.

This negative pattern of interaction needs to be short-circuited as soon as it is identified in order to avoid long-term damage. You can do this by softening your tone of voice and acknowledging your partner's point of view. Making a commitment not to use shared information as weapons and taking a time-out to de-escalate can also help defuse the situation.

2. Invalidation. This is the "put-down" style of conflict. It involves one or both spouses making negative comments about the other's personality, character, intellect, or feelings. Whether intentional or unintentional, the end result is a lower sense of self-esteem on the part of the targeted spouse. Invalidation can take many forms, such as telling your spouse that his or her thoughts or feelings are wrong or stupid; ignoring or criticizing something positive your spouse was attempting to do; or interrupting or talking over your spouse in a conversation.

Preventing this negative pattern from continuing in your relationship involves being willing to acknowledge and show respect for each other's differing viewpoints. It can also be helpful to express appreciation to each other for positive efforts made and affirm that "different" does not mean "wrong."

3. Withdrawal and avoidance. This is the "I'm out of here" style of dealing with conflicts. This occurs when one spouse is unwilling to engage in or stay with an important discussion to the point of resolution. The withdrawal may be physical (getting up and walking out of the room) or emotional ("shutting down" and going quiet during a discussion). Both are attempts to remove yourself from the conversation. Avoidance is another way to show unwillingness to engage in a particular conversation. You might use distractions, change the subject, or simply make yourself unavailable. The spouse who brought up the topic pushes harder, and the avoiding spouse withdraws even more. You are both caught in a negative spiral.

Changing this pattern involves first and foremost recognizing your tendencies either to pursue or withdraw and then working together to come at important discussions in a more constructive manner. Understanding that your actions will cause reactions in your spouse can help you better choose how you want to act.

4. Negative interpretations. This is the "you're bad" pattern of dealing with conflicts. This occurs when one spouse has formed an excessively negative interpretation of the other. This spouse consistently believes that the motives, opinions, and actions of the other are more negative than is actually the case. As humans, we have a tendency to look for evidence that confirms what we already believe to be true. So if you determine within yourself that your spouse is "bad," then you will look for evidence to support that belief. While you are doing that, you may overlook any evidence to the contrary and therefore miss the positive aspects of your spouse.

Overcoming this pattern lies mainly in the hands of the one who's holding the negative view. No one can make you change how you interpret your spouse's actions except you. You may want to start by openly and realistically evaluating whether you are overemphasizing the negative traits in your spouse. The best way to overcome this pattern is simply to commit yourself to looking for and finding the positive in your spouse.

Now that you can identify the unhealthy patterns of conflictual interactions and what you may have been doing wrong, it is time to show you how to do it right. The rest of this chapter focuses on how to correct and resolve the problems within your relationship in a healthy manner. You will learn how to fight in a way that does not destroy intimacy, but rather actually builds it. You will learn both what to do and what not to do in this process of fair fighting. So let's get started.

How to Have a FAIR Fight

Let's look at the components that are absolutely necessary to resolve conflict and reach greater intimacy.

What is FAIR Fighting?
F: Forgiving attitude
A: Applying ECHO conversation skills
I: "I" messages
R: Resolution

F
Forgiving attitude

You may wonder why this is the first key component. Doesn't forgiveness come at the end, after all the hurt of a fight? I believe that if it comes first, you actually may be able to avoid some of the pain that conflicts can cause. Although you may ask for and give forgiveness at the end of the conflict, the willingness to forgive must be present even before the conflict begins.

Imagine, before the conflict begins, saying to yourself, "I know we are about to enter into a difficult discussion. I know that we both want to see this resolved. But because we are human and we make mistakes, I know that either one of us may say something hurtful. I know we are both trying to avoid doing this, but if we do slip up, I know I am willing to forgive my spouse or to ask for forgiveness and do my best to move on." Do you think you would enter the discussion with a different perspective? Do you think, just maybe, your attitude would soften and the possible slip-ups would not seem quite so harmful? I do. I know that the attitude I enter a discussion with is usually intensified as the discussion continues. If I start out defensive, I seem to hear things in a more negative light, and I become more defensive. However, if I enter with a softness and willingness to forgive, I seem better able to hear what Jim is trying to say and better able to look past things that may come out wrong.

An important point here is to avoid assigning motives to your spouse's statements. This may be difficult to do. Once you enter a conflict, you may become self-protective. You believe there are good reasons for your own behavior. If you make a mistake in the way you say something, you say, "I didn't mean that." And, of course, you expect your spouse to forget your mistake and move on. After all, it was not intentional, right? How often do you give your spouse the same benefit of the doubt? It is too easy to assign an evil motive or a bad attitude as the reason for his or her behavior. And if your spouse says something in a way that hurts you, you just know it was "on purpose." Beware: This self-protective approach usually becomes self-defeating in the fight for greater intimacy.

If there is an occasion when either of you becomes hurtful in a conflict, it is essential that you admit to this and actively seek your spouse's forgiveness. Put your mistake and apology into words and ask your spouse to forgive you. ("I am sorry that I compared you to your mother. That was wrong. Please forgive me.") Don't just say, "I'm sorry," and assume your partner knows what you are apologizing for. Remember also to grant the forgiveness verbally.

A
Applying ECHO conversation skills

The second key component to FAIR fighting is the ability to listen to what is being said. The listening technique called ECHO conversations will help you in that process (see chapter 7). Being able to listen attentively and really understand what is being said is one of the most valuable tools you can ever learn. It is necessary for healthy communication about any topic, but it is particularly essential when the two of you disagree. Part of ECHO conversations include a time where you repeat to your spouse what you heard him or her saying. This part can be especially difficult during an argument because you will be saying with your own mouth something that you disagree with. And on top of that, you have to do so without inserting your own thoughts, opinions, corrections, or solutions. Talk about hard! Conflict-resolution skills will take some practice, but they are definitely worth all the effort. Conversations that become conflictual usually do so because one or both parties do not feel heard and understood. Using ECHO conversation skills will help each of you feel you have been heard and understood and will likely reduce the number of unresolved conflicts within your relationship. Remember, having your spouse understand you does not necessarily mean he or she will agree with you. Your focus should not be on getting your spouse to agree with you. Rather, focus on getting *each* of you to *understand* what the other is thinking and feeling. You may never agree, but you will most likely be able to gain some understanding of the other's point of view. ECHO conversations will help you clarify what is being said and identify the true issues the two of you need to address. Once that is accomplished, the possible solutions to the real issues seem easier to find, and greater intimacy is the result. As you apply these skills of FAIR fighting, seek more to understand than to be understood.

I
"I" messages

This could be one of the most beneficial tools you can learn for conflict resolution. "I" messages are one of the best ways to express anger (or any feeling) appropriately. When you use "I" messages, you do not attack the other person in a dirty, mudslinging, win-at-all-costs battle. Instead, you simply express your own feelings about a situation. ("I feel neglected when you don't spend time with me.") These are your feelings and yours only, and therefore others cannot challenge them. When you use "I" statements, you take responsibility for your feeling. You do not blame or judge the other person for making you feel this way. ("You always ignore me! You don't even care about me!")

"I" messages not only help us identify our feelings and make us responsible for them, they also empower us. They help us realize that we are not helpless or powerless to change things. "You" messages, in comparison, make others responsible for our feelings, blame others for the problem, and therefore make us helpless to bring about changes. Using "you" statements to blame others for how we are feeling puts not only the responsibility of the problem on the other person, but also the responsibility for the solution. When you blame others, you are saying, "Since the problem is your fault, then only you can change it." We tend to blame others while seeing ourselves as blameless (most likely untrue). The problem is that you also end up seeing yourself as helpless to resolve the situation (also probably untrue). Let's look at a few examples of "you" vs. "I" statements. As we do this, try to evaluate how you may be using "you" messages to blame or judge your spouse, or to avoid taking responsibility for your own feelings.

"You" statements	"I" statements
"You make me so mad."	"I feel angry when you _____."
"You are a lazy, good-for-nothing jerk."	"I feel taken advantage of when you don't help out around the house."
"You had better stop flirting."	"I feel insecure in our relationship when you flirt."
"All you ever do is spend money."	"I feel nervous when you spend money before the bills are paid."

R
Resolution

The final key concept of FAIR fighting is the importance of reaching a resolution. Often conflicts are started but never really finished. Why is that? There are several possible reasons, including walking away, getting sidetracked, bringing up irrelevant topics, throwing up the past, and being interrupted. The result of unresolved conflict is often harbored anger and frustration for one or both parties.

Take the following example and consider how often something like this happens in your relationship.

"Why didn't you call and tell me you were going to be late?" (Defensiveness is evident and conflict begins.)

"I tried to call ..." (Another topic is introduced.) "... but I couldn't get through because you were on the Internet like you always are." (Now both are defensive and another topic is added.)

"Well, maybe I wouldn't be on the Net so much if you were ever here to talk to."

And on and on it goes. Where it will stop, no one knows. But likely it will be with one or both withdrawing or walking away. These irrelevant topics are likely unresolved conflicts from the past. Not only does everyone involved become hurt and angry, but now you have lost track of the original issue, which simply becomes one more of the many other topics that are unresolved and are now available to be thrown up in the next conflict.

Do your best to keep the conversation focused on the original topic until it has been adequately resolved. Then, and only then, move on to additional topics that the two of you may need to address. Be careful to not overload your spouse with grievances. Now that you have the skills to resolve conflicts, you can address them a couple at a time. Eventually, you can reach a place where there are no unresolved issues to throw at each other.

If emotions begin to escalate to the point that either of you is unable to be civil and rational, then call a time-out. Either party can call a time-out. The purpose is to calm down. This is not an escape route; it is simply a break in the conversation. Agree on a time to reconvene, and continue the discussion once both of you have had some time apart and can think about the topic more reasonably. The amount of time apart will vary depending on the level of emotions. It may be as little as ten minutes, but I would suggest it not be longer than twenty-four hours. The longer you wait, the less likely it is that you come back to the topic and resolve it. Use this time to appropriately release any excessive emotions you might be experiencing. You can do this effectively through physical safety valves (such as walking, jogging, cleaning, or other physical activity) or through emotional safety valves (such as crying, journaling, or praying). Once you feel your emotions are back in line, focus on what you think and feel about the topic and how you would like to see it resolved. When the time-out is over, you will be ready to continue the discussion to resolution.

Now that you understand the four key components to FAIR fighting, it is time to review the actual rules that will help make these concepts become a reality in your marriage. Below is a list of the basic rules for resolving conflict. (For a more detailed description of these, see my book *Discovering the Treasure of Marriage*.)[5] These are some of the basic things you will need to agree to for your conflicts to proceed toward the point of resolution and greater intimacy.

Rules for FAIR Fighting

1. **Clearly identify the problem or issue.** Be specific when you introduce a problem.
2. **Don't just complain.** Ask for a reasonable change that will relieve the problem.
3. **Always be willing to compromise.** Remember that your partner's view of reality and the problem may be just as real as yours, even though you differ.
4. **Confine yourself to one issue at a time.** Don't overload your partner with several grievances at once; avoid switching to another issue before the first is resolved.
5. **Arrange a specific time and place to work it through.**

6. **Attack the problem, not the person.** Dwell on behaviors, not on personality or characteristics. Never put labels on your spouse.
7. **Avoid using absolutes.** Words like "always" or "never" result in defensiveness.
8. **Don't assume.** Don't assume you know what the other is thinking or feeling.
9. **Forget the past and stay with the here and now.** Don't bring up old hurts.
10. **Admit when you are wrong.** Be graciously silent when you are right.
11. **Think before you speak.** Pause to consider your thoughts and feelings before speaking.
12. **Don't hit below the belt.** Avoid criticizing the unchangeable and pushing on those old sore spots. Know your partner's emotional limits and stay within those limits.
13. **Be ready and willing to forgive.**
14. **Apply ECHO conversation skills.**
15. **Use "I" messages.** These present your grievance in a nonattacking way and make it clear that you accept responsibility for your feelings.

Coming Up Next ...

Are you and your spouse fighting against each other more than against the outside world? Internal conflict and turmoil can rip apart the very fabric of the parenting team. Working together as a team is especially important during the parenting years of marriage. If you are not a unified team, your opponents (the kids) will have the upper hand and will be capable of dividing and therefore conquering your team. Learning to work together as a team is the focus of the next chapter.

CHAPTER EIGHT

WHOSE TEAM ARE YOU ON?

Essential Element 8: Teamwork

I heard it said somewhere: "Getting good players is easy. Getting them to play together is the hard part." Boy, that's the truth. Marriages and parenting teams all over the world are made up of good players who have good skills but are failing miserably in both marriage and parenting. Why is that? That's what this chapter is all about—learning how to be a team with your spouse when it comes to parenting. We will discuss the major components of teamwork and the importance of healthy boundaries, which all work together to help you reach your common goal of a healthy marriage and family.

Let's start by discussing the four major components of teamwork: having a game plan, presenting a united front, cooperating, and boundaries.

Teamwork Requires a Game Plan

Before and during a game, a winning team takes time to create, study, and revise its game plan. Part of the preparation before the game involves brainstorming and creating a playbook. Team members choose from the plays in this book as they develop a game plan. The playbook has many different plays because there will be many different situations during the game. But all the plays in the playbook are ones the team has agreed on and accepted as appropriate and ready for use. As you become more aware of your opponent, you will choose the plays from the playbook that you believe to be most effective. Each opponent is different. Each has strengths, weaknesses, and strategies. So plays that work against one opponent may not be effective against another.

As members of a parenting team, you will need to develop your own game plan. As you parent, you will need to have a variety of options to choose from. Discuss these with your spouse and agree upon the basic set of "plays," or interventions, that make up your parenting game plan. If there is a particular suggestion or style of parenting that one of you is not comfortable with, take additional time to discuss it. You will not agree on every specific way you choose to raise your children. If the differences are minor, you may be able to work out a compromise or trade-off. For example, if one of you is concerned about the amount of television your children watch and the other thinks television is fine, you may be able to compromise on a selected amount of television or particular set of programs. However, if the differences are more extreme and have an emotional component for one of the parents, you may be better off deciding not to include that particular intervention in your playbook. For example, if your spouse is strongly opposed to physical punishment because of being abused as a child, regardless of how you feel about this, you should be willing to not use this form of punishment and work to find alternatives.

Children Are Different from Day One

Another reason to have a variety of plays available is that each of your children is a different opponent and will come to the field with different skills and strategies. Each child will require different maneuvers on your part. Let me share with you how this has played out within our family.

When Taffeta was born, the delivery room (and probably the entire hospital) knew it. She seemed to come out walking, talking, and smoking a cigar. She was as independent as any infant could be, and I am sure those cries were nothing more than her shouting orders at the staff and asking the doctor what took so long. She was strong-willed and argumentative from the beginning and has always been determined to blaze her own path. She has spent the past twelve years honing her verbal and intellectual skills (not that they needed much honing, considering that by the age of two she succeeded in talking her way out of time-out). She has come to the point that she could successfully argue, defend, and generally talk her way out of just about anything, if she were allowed to.

Then there was Tiara. She also made herself known in the delivery room, but in a much different way. She was not going to capture the attention of the staff by shouting orders or just looking cute. No, that would not have been good enough for this little attention-seeking beauty with a flare for the dramatic. She was going to make an entrance to end all entrances and one that was sure to grab her that extra dose of attention that many middle children seem to seek. Her delivery was just as intense, spellbinding, emotional, and dramatic as she is. She (along with her mother) barely escaped the claws of death in this, her first but definitely not last, appearance on center stage. Since her first stage appearance nine years ago, this little actress has continued to refine her acting abilities. She is now quite skilled at creating tears on command (her command that is) and at convincing any listening audience that she is sure to die if forced to remain in her room for even one second more.

And then there was Talon. What was left after following those two acts? Was baby number three really going to be that different? Or maybe just a smaller version of one of his sisters? If we had figured out how to parent despite the efforts of these two master manipulators, the attorney and the actress, we were sure we could handle anything. But then God threw us a curve ball. In the delivery room full of staff, this little man (and I call him "little man" because at nine pounds he was not a baby) captured just as much attention as his predecessors but in an unexpected way. He was simply the cutest thing to ever grace the earth with his presence. He was soft, gentle, and snuggly. His modus operandi was to flash his baby blues and melt your heart, which would render you completely helpless. Which is exactly what he has been doing for the past five years—rendering all of our well-developed and hard-nosed parenting strategies useless. How does he accomplish this? When one of us seems to get upset with him and starts to punish, he will quickly reach up for a hug, flash a smile, and say, "I wuv you the mostest!" And we can't seem to remember what we were about to do.

As you can see, all three of these children have been different from day one. And, as they have grown, they have challenged our parenting team in completely different ways. The game plan we developed with Taffeta had to be completely revamped when Tiara arrived, and then again when Talon came on the field. Our game plan has continued to change as the children have grown and developed new strategies. Our opponents are different and constantly changing. One of the skills our parenting team must learn is flexibility. The better we communicate and keep each other informed about how we see things working, the more likely it is that our team will continue to be effective on the field.

Teamwork Requires Presenting a United Front

If you hope to win the big game, you have to be unified in your efforts. You will come up against a formidable opponent whose main goal (other than getting his or her own way) is to divide and conquer your team. If you hope to survive you must become unified in all you do—lock arms (and hearts) and stand firm together!

Being unified means understanding that this is not a one-person show. There is no room for hot-dogging or ball-hogging in this game. If you go out on your own to tackle your opponent, you will likely find yourself without backup when you most need it. So commit to each other that you will stick to the game plan and work on parenting together.

The strength of your union will show in the day-to-day application of the game plan you agree on. No matter how much the two of you agree to make your parenting and discipline decisions together, there will be times where one of you is put in a position of having to make an on-the-spot decision. Although your basic, agreed-upon guidelines will help in making that decision, that is no guarantee that you will end up choosing what your spouse would have chosen. Disagreements are bound to occur. How you handle these situations will tell both you and your children just how united the two of you really are.

Here are some suggestions to help keep up a united front:

1. Don't argue about parenting or discipline decisions in front of the children. This includes situations where you are both present and need to intervene with your child, as well as situations where one of you had to make a decision without the other present. If you are both present and struggling to come up with an agreeable solution, call a time-out. The two of you should retreat to the sidelines and discuss this situation privately. During that private time, work on a solution you can agree on. When you return to your child, present the decision with a united front.

2. Support the decisions your spouse makes. Let's say you were gone for the afternoon and came home to find that your spouse has banned your son from the computer for two weeks for what seems to you like a minor offense. Don't say, "Two weeks? You have to be kidding!" All that does is undermine your spouse's authority and inform your son that there is a weak link in the parenting team. Even if you do not agree on how the situation was handled, show support of your spouse in front of the child. Take time later to talk about it privately and hear the whole story. You may realize that you can now better understand the outcome.

If you still are not in agreement with your spouse, you have two choices. First, you may decide within yourself whether this is really a battle worth fighting. Is the world going to end if you decide to support and follow through with the decision already made? Probably not. So unless the situation is really going to cause some long-term damage, seriously consider supporting it.

The second option is to express to your spouse the reasons for your disagreement. I would recommend using the conflict-management skills presented in chapter 7 to help you work toward a resolution and compromise. Once the two of you have reached a mutually agreed-upon resolution, present that to your child as a team. Let your child know that the two of you have discussed this and have decided together to overturn the previous decision.

3. Don't allow your kids to play you against each other. "Mom said I could play next door with Megan." "Dad told me it was okay to listen to that CD." Sound familiar? We have all experienced the "Mom-said-Dad-said" strategy from our children (and if we're honest, we all tried it ourselves when we were young). This is an obvious "divide and conquer" technique that can cause considerable damage to the parenting team. If you fall into the trap of simply believing that the other parent actually did say whatever your child claims, you likely will find yourself arguing with your spouse before you even check it out. "I can't believe you told Scott he could listen to that CD. You know we agreed to no hard rock." And before your spouse can confirm or deny saying that, you two are off and running (and Scott is listening to his CD).

Kids may keep asking until they get the answer they want. Many children will ask one parent to do something. If the child does not like the answer, it's off to ask the other parent. Without knowing that you have already said no, your spouse may say yes. Now having gotten the "right" answer, your child gleefully goes about doing whatever he or she had been told not to do (at least by one of you). This not only shows your children that your team is not unified, it also likely will be the source of additional conflicts between the two of you.

The best defense against this strategy is a simple, "Let's go check with your mom (or dad) about this." Once your children know that you will be checking in with each other and making decisions together, you will have rendered this technique useless.

Teamwork Requires Cooperation

Successful teams are the ones whose members have learned to work together to accomplish their mutual goals. They understand and respect the importance of each player's contribution to the team. They have learned that they can accomplish so much more when they do it together than if they were each trying to go it alone. Successful teams have learned to cooperate.

Coparenting happens when the parenting team decides to cooperate in all areas of parenting. It means doing things together and accepting that you are both equally responsible for raising your children. When you coparent, you work together to set family rules and consequences, decide on family responsibilities, and manage the daily requirements of the home. Anything that involves parenting involves both parents.

The concept of coparenting has grown over the past few

decades as more and more families have become dual-income families. With both parents working outside the home, couples have started to divide the requirements of running the home more evenly. More and more fathers participate in household responsibilities such as cooking, cleaning, laundry, and childcare. But even if you are one of those families where one parent (not always the mom anymore) works at home while the other works outside the home, you will still benefit from learning to cooperate in the parenting process.

One of the most important points to remember as you work to develop a coparenting team is to avoid comparing yourself to other teams. Each parenting team is unique and holds within it a unique set of strengths and weaknesses. When you realize that no two teams are alike, you will understand why comparing your team to any other team is just asking for trouble. What you find that seems to work best for your team may not work for others. And what they discover works for them may fail miserably within your home. There is no "right" or "best" way to play this game, except to know and then capitalize on your own specific strengths.

Focus on the strengths and talents God has created within your team. When you focus on being who God has asked you to be and doing that to the best of your ability, you will become the best spouse and parent you can possibly be.

When I had my first child there was no question as to whether I would return to work. I was in the middle of my internship; if I had any hope of graduating, I had to get back to work as soon as I could. Although it was difficult leaving Taffeta, I soon adjusted to juggling child and career because I loved both. However, this decision was not quite as easy three years later, after having Tiara.

It was not that I had decided I did not like my work anymore, because I did. Helping people get through their problems and improve their lives is my passion. And, left to my own devices, I would never have given my return to work a second thought.

Unfortunately, we are seldom left to our own devices. As has almost always been the case for me, the majority of my close friends were people I had met at church. I was surrounded with strong Christian wives and mothers whom I admired tremendously—and who were practically all stay-at-home moms. As I interacted with them more and more, I began to feel guilty. I am not saying they purposely took it upon themselves to enlighten me as to the error of my ways. But I started to feel it in the way they would talk to me. I heard things such as:

"Don't you just hate having to leave your girls and go back to work?"

"I don't think I could ever feel comfortable leaving my kids in a daycare."

"I hope you don't have to miss out on Tiara's first steps."

"Money may be tight for us, but raising my kids myself is worth it."

Before long I started doubting that I was doing the right thing. Here were all these wonderful Christian women who knew that staying home and raising their children was the best thing in the world. I started thinking that maybe I just was not as good a Christian, or that God would not be able to bless me if I went back to work.

I talked with Jim about this, but he didn't take me very seriously because he knew how much I loved my job and that God had called me to it. But I still was not convinced, and I continued to worry (and pray "a little") about it. It was not until after I actually had Tiara and was at home recovering that I finally made my decision.

Tiara was about four weeks old, and I had spent the previous four weeks cooped up at home with a new baby and a three-year-old. I kept trying to tell myself this was supposed to be the most fun and fulfilling thing I had ever done. As a matter of fact, I kept calling those "good Christian friends" of mine to help remind me that this was the "right" thing to do. Then it happened. The total meltdown. I had spent the day juggling everything I could: nursing, washing dishes, reading books, doing laundry, nursing, changing diapers, playing Barbies, nursing ... (and that was all before noon). I have no idea what the last straw was, but the next thing I remember, there were three tired, cranky, and confused girls (Taffeta, Tiara, and me) sitting on the floor crying uncontrollably. Once I could catch my breath and calm the other two down, I picked up the phone to call a "friend." When she answered, I half yelled and half cried into the receiver, "If I *ever* tell you that I'm going to be a stay-at-home mom, just remind me that I am *no good at it!*" Then and there I knew that God had not created me to be a stay-at-home mom, and I realized that I had been comparing myself to others, not to God's plan for my life.

As you can see from my own life, it is important to not try to make your family fit a particular mold. God has carved you out uniquely to fit His plan for you. As long as you are trying to squeeze into a mold set for someone else you will be discontented and unhappy and unfulfilled. I encourage you to spend some time seeking God and His plan for you and your family, and then do your best to work within that plan.

Now that you have the information you need to help you create a game plan, present a united front, and work together as a team, let's turn our attention to the last major component of teamwork—developing healthy boundaries

Know What You're Good At and Do It

A good team has to learn to work together in such a way that it utilizes each member's strengths and supports each member's weaknesses. Although each member may serve as a backup for the others, all the members know what their main roles are. When the game is on, each team member should be doing the assigned task, not something that someone else should be doing. You do not want your quarterback going around making sure everyone has had something to drink or helping the other team find its locker room or selling souvenirs. That is not his job any more than it is the concession server's job to throw the football. Learning what your particular job is and what you are responsible for in your life and your family is part of what is called "boundaries." Let's take a minute to discuss what boundaries are and how best to apply them for yourself and your family.

What Are Boundaries?

Boundaries are lines (often invisible) that define where one thing ends and another begins, like the property lines that separate your property from your neighbors'. This line may have become visible by the construction of a fence. Often, fences serve as boundaries for children to help keep them safe. A fence shows them how far they can venture and reminds them that if they go beyond that boundary, they are going beyond their safety zone.

Boundaries also remind us of what we are and are not responsible for. Your property boundaries tell you that you are responsible for the things inside your boundary lines but not outside of them. Let's say you decide to sit inside your house all summer and have no consideration for the fact that your yard needs to be mowed. It won't be long before you look out your window and see knee-high grass. You may be saying to yourself, "What's wrong with those neighbors of mine? Why haven't they gotten over here and taken care of my yard for me?"

Now, I know that may sound ridiculous, but that is exactly what many people do in their relationships. They sit back and expect someone else to be responsible for the things that really they should be taking care of themselves. I'm sure you have met one of those people (or maybe you are one) who seems to want or need everyone around them to fix their problems for them. Although many of us would be willing to help once or twice, we do not want to be in a situation of doing it for them continually.

I heard about a woman who attended a local church and went to the pastor to ask for some financial help. She was a single mother of two school-age kids, had lost her job several weeks earlier, and was about to have her electricity turned off. Of course he helped her out and she was grateful. The next month, she approached him again for help, stating that she did not have enough money to pay the rent. She still did not have a job because she was "waiting for just the right one to come along." The pastor agreed to help her out one more time and asked her to attend a money-management class they were having at the church. She agreed but never attended. Her Sunday school class was also helping this family out by providing some meals and groceries and helping her children out with some school supplies. The woman continued to be extremely grateful, but she did not seem to be making any steps to change her situation.

One day, a friend from her Sunday school class offered to drive her around to some possible job sites so she could put in some applications. The woman graciously refused, stating that she had a lunch date that day. It was becoming clear to the people of this church that this woman was in no hurry to start taking care of herself as long as they were taking care of everything for her. They decided to inform her that they were not going to be able to continue to help financially, but were willing to do what they could to help her find a job. The woman became upset, started crying, and told the pastor that he just didn't understand or maybe didn't really care about her and her children or he would be there for her. He continued to try to explain how he and the church would continue to support her, but she just got mad and walked out. A few weeks later he got a call from a pastor friend across town stating that this woman was at their church asking for help.

This is the kind of person who sits in the house all summer and lets someone else take care of the yard.

Now let's look at the other side of the fence. Let's say you are out mowing your lawn and notice that your neighbors' yard needs to be mowed; so you go into their yard and take care of it. I'm sure your neighbors appreciate that and may even tell you so. What if the next week the same thing happens? Since you liked how your neighbors said thank you, you decide to do it again. What if the next week your neighbors ask you to do it because you did such a great job the last time? Before you know it, the neighbors are expecting you to take care of their yard all the time. You had just wanted to do something nice, but because you can't seem to say no and because you like to feel needed, now you feel responsible for both your yard and theirs.

Some people really do behave this way in their relationships. They take on responsibilities that are not theirs as a way of being nice, hoping it will make other people like them. They cannot seem to say no when asked to do something they really do not want to do. Their need to feel needed, important, and liked overrides their need to take care of themselves. These people often end up overwhelmed and exhausted but have convinced themselves that at least everyone likes them. And then there are always those people who are more than willing to take advantage of the neighbor who is willing to take responsibility for everyone else's stuff.

One of the most stable and yet unhealthy relationships is the one between the neighbor who wants to stay inside all summer and the one who is willing to take care of that neighbor's yard. This is not healthy for either of them. One will start building resentments about being taken advantage of, and the other will never learn to be responsible for her or his own life.

The healthiest relationship is the one between two neighbors who both understand and respect the boundary line. These are the neighbors who are each capable and willing to take care of what is within their fence. They know and trust that the other neighbor is willing to do the same. When all involved take care of themselves and what they are responsible for, and do not cross boundaries without permission, healthy, secure relationships develop.

Boundaries Are Important in Marriage and Parenting

Once you understand how boundaries can help define healthy relationships, you will understand how important they can be in the marriage and parenting relationship. As you grow in your understanding of each other, you can identify each of your strengths and weaknesses. Once you identify a particular strength in one of you, work together to best use that strength. And when you identify a weak area in one of you, the two of you together should work to compensate for that. A team functions at its best when it uses its members' strengths. Remember, the healthiest relationships are those in which each person's responsibilities are clearly identified and defined.

Coming Up Next ...

We are about to reach the last (but definitely not least) of the nine essential elements of a strong and healthy marriage–parenting team—sexual intimacy. Although sex may at times seem a thing of the past once we become parents, it doesn't have to be that way. Yes, there are concessions to make at different stages of the parenting season, but a strong physical relationship is important to a strong and growing marriage.

CHAPTER NINE

JUST BETWEEN YOU AND ME

Essential Element 9: Physical Intimacy

By the end of the day, I'm so exhausted that I can't think about anything except sleep. I have been going nonstop since about six o'clock in the morning with two toddlers climbing on top of me all day. Please don't get me wrong. I love my kids; it's just that sometimes I feel like I don't even know who I am anymore. I really miss my husband and the quiet times we used to have together. And, believe me, I know he's missing me. Just the other night he came home from work saying he was exhausted from a long day. Although I felt bad for him, part of me was actually relieved, because to me that meant that he would probably be ready for bed when I was. And that's the minute we get the kids to sleep. But that's not how it went.

"Once the kids were asleep, I asked him if he was ready for bed.

He took that to mean something totally different than I did. His eyes and face brightened up and he jumped up off the couch and said, 'I thought you'd never ask!' That's when I knew he had sex on his mind. I looked at him and said, 'I thought you said you were exhausted?' His reply was to pick me up and swing me around, saying, 'I did. But sweetie, I'm never too exhausted to make love to you.'

"How can that be? When I say I'm exhausted, I mean, I'm dead-dog tired. As a matter of fact, I could never have even thought of jumping up off the couch the way he did. All I wanted to do was just hit the bed and sleep for a week. And there's my loving husband expecting me to have the energy for sex."

That's how one young woman I interviewed answered my question about how children have affected her sex life. And she was not alone. Many of the responses I got were variations of her comments. Several people started to laugh and say, "Sex life? What's that?" Men and women alike shared that sex seemed to be the most changed part of their marriage since they had children. But it didn't stop with just sex; they also reported experiencing less touching in general. One husband said, "I can't even remember the last time we sat on the couch alone to cuddle. There always seems to be a kid between us." Another couple shared that they couldn't recall the last time they "really kissed"; what kissing they did seemed to be just like the kisses they gave the kids at bedtime.

Although just about everyone I talked to described their sex life as less satisfactory than it used to be, they also all seemed to express the need to be flexible with each other through these times. They expressed knowing they loved each other and yet were having to find some new ways to express this love. Physical intimacy was still an important need for each of them, but the frequency and spontaneity of these intimate times together had definitely changed. Many of the suggestions in this chapter came from couples just like you, who are out there trying to stay connected while raising their kids.

The biggest encouragement I can give you is that physical intimacy does not have to become a thing of the past once the children arrive. I know this is a major fear of many parents, but the need for a couple to stay connected physically is just as strong through the parenting years as any other time. However, these years do present their own set of challenges. Finding new ways to connect physically, scheduling time to be alone together, and conserving energy for lovemaking are all part of the package of staying connected physically.

Taking Shortcuts

When we become overwhelmed with life and responsibilities, we have a tendency to take shortcuts. The purpose of shortcuts is to save time and energy; this can be very beneficial in many areas of our busy lives as parents. (I will give you some specific ways to take shortcuts in chapter 12.) Taking shortcuts in meal preparation, house cleaning, and daily chores is great. However, when it comes to your marriage, and especially your sexual relationship, this is not the place for taking shortcuts.

Taking shortcuts means taking out some of the least-needed or noticeable parts of a task in order to focus on the more essential parts with the limited energy that you have. For example, in cleaning house, shortcuts might mean ignoring the dust in the corners and under the bed and focusing on what is easily visible. Or you might stuff some things into the closet and shut the doors to some rooms. These shortcuts give the appearance of all the work being done and tend to meet a basic need of having a clean, organized home. When we have limited time and energy to get a task done, we prioritize the parts of it and do the most important ones. The problem with this occurs when the husband and wife do not agree on what is the "most important" part. And they seldom do.

Jim and I decided one Saturday afternoon that we would invite a few friends over for a casual dinner later that same day. After the calls were made and the specifics arranged, we started considering what needed to be done before our guests would arrive in just a few short hours. About that time, I realized that maybe we had not thought this thing through too well. Instead of getting up and cleaning house that morning, we had elected to sleep in, lounge around like bums, and just hang out with the kids. Now, don't get me wrong—that was great! But it is not what I would have been doing had I planned to have a dinner party later that day.

The house was a disaster! And I do not mean just cluttered with toys and kid stuff—I mean a disaster! I started to calculate how long I thought it would take to get it presentable and soon realized that the answer was way too much time! I had a brief moment of panic and then realized that we could get by with getting the main level cleaned up and just hoping no one would need to go upstairs. That seemed doable, and I was sure if we all pitched in we could get it done. About that time I saw Jim coming down the stairs in his old work shorts and torn-up tennis shoes. I knew we had a problem. These were not his housecleaning clothes—what could he be thinking? We have guests coming over and here he comes all decked out in his "mow-the-yard" clothes. He's got to be crazy if he thinks he has time to mow the yard! But before I had a chance to say a word, he saw the look on my face and started explaining himself. "I've got to work on the yard. I haven't had time to mow it in almost two weeks and it looks awful. We can't have company with it looking like that!"

Things didn't get any prettier from there. I couldn't believe he was not planning to stay inside and help get the house in order. Who cares about the yard? We weren't going to be out there. But all he could think about was how bad the yard looked and how that would be the first thing our friends would see. The yard was a reflection on him and therefore his higher priority. The house was more of a reflection on me and therefore my higher priority. We both knew that we would have to take some shortcuts to get the "most important" parts done. To me, those shortcuts included shoving things into closets and closing doors. To Jim, they included skipping the trimming and not washing off the sidewalk. Our thoughts about what could be left undone were thoroughly different. What I considered priority and essential was nowhere close to what he determined to be essential.

As you can see, husbands and wives are different in how they think and prioritize even the little things. And if you think we are different in these areas, you should see how different we are when it comes to sex.

What's the "Most Important" Part?

The differences between men and women are talked about everywhere and are evident in every area of our lives. But nowhere are these differences more obvious than in the bedroom. There seem to be no similarities, except that we both are absolutely confused by the other's views, responses, and needs when it comes to sex. Knowing and accepting these differences will help you understand why your marriage, and especially your sex life, is not the place to take shortcuts. The purpose of shortcuts in the other areas of your life is to save time and energy that can then be given to the marriage. As a couple, you must learn to save some of the time and energy allotted to you as a couple for the sexual part of your relationship. And this goes double for women! Why? Because men are naturally better at conserving energy for sex; when they say they are exhausted, they really mean they have no energy for anything— except sex. On the other hand, a woman is much more likely to use up every spare ounce of energy she has before saying she's exhausted, and when she says it, she really means she has no energy for anything. Period! So, women, listen up! Make a conscious effort to reserve some of your energy for special times with your husband.

Almost every aspect of your relationship will experience some changes once children arrive, and your physical relationship is no exception. But how these different areas change is up to you. Although you may not have time and energy for long, uninterrupted lovemaking sessions, you can make time to connect physically. The important key here is to understand that you each need and desire different things from your sexual relationship. Then you can work toward a healthy middle ground that will help keep you both satisfied. If you do not discuss these differences, you will be tempted to take shortcuts in some areas of your physical relationship to allow more time for the more "essential" parts. But what happens if what you determine to be unnecessary and unimportant is one of the most important parts for your spouse?

Let's take an example. You may decide that foreplay is not really all that important, and so you decide to leave it out, or at least cut back the amount of time devoted to it. In your mind, you are just helping you both adjust to having limited time for sex. Taking this "shortcut" is saving time and energy that could be better used for more "important" activities. And besides, if you take too long with the foreplay, you end up being interrupted by the kids. And that could mean never getting to that "most important" part. This may sound like a great solution until you find out that foreplay is the most essential element of sex to your spouse. Your spouse may need any extra time you have to be spent engaging in foreplay. This may be what helps him or her begin to put the rest of the world (including the kids) on hold and start to feel close, connected, and sexually aroused. As a matter of fact, on some days, foreplay may be all your spouse needs. He or she may not mind at all if the two of you get interrupted before "the act" as long as you have spent time touching, snuggling, and caressing.

Where each of you may decide to take shortcuts in your physical relationship may actually be harmful to your relationship. If you know that you are different in your physical needs, is there really any hope that you can stay connected sexually with so little time and energy available? Of course there is, as long as the two of you are willing to identify and understand your differences and then commit to saving some of your time and energy for this important part of your relationship. Here are a few suggestions to help you think about how to stay connected physically while you have kids in the home:

1. Just two in a bed. Kids have their own beds; use them.
2. Put a lock on the bedroom door and use it.
3. Get a white-noise maker or radio and place it close to your bedroom door.
4. Hug for thirty seconds.
5. Kiss and hold it at least fifteen seconds.
6. Start saving your change for a special adult-only evening or weekend.
7. Get a set of non-mommy, non-daddy sleep-wear and wear it often.
8. Send a suggestive note, email, or voice mail.
9. Flirt with each other.
10. Always have the essentials and a few extras readily available (such as lubricant, effective birth control, massage oil, bubble bath, candles, CD of love songs, and so forth).

Sex—One of His Essentials for Life

Let's look at a man's core makeup as it relates to sex. Sexual activity for a man can be likened to his view of money. He absolutely loves it. He is willing to work for it (usually), but prefers it to come easily. He seems to never have enough of it. Even if he were to receive a large "bonus" today, he would very much like to have another one tomorrow and the next day and the next day. He can never seem to get enough to totally satisfy his desire. It is what his world revolves around, and he truly believes he cannot live without it.

This is really not far from the truth for most men. Sex is a vital part of their existence. They are sexual beings through and through. Husbands think about sex more often than their wives do, are aroused much more quickly and spontaneously than we are, and place a much higher priority on the act of sex than women do. They are aroused visually (even when their wives feel anything but sexy), and acts of affection are really defined as foreplay in their minds.

Their ability to separate events in their minds makes it possible for them to be "in the mood" anytime and anywhere (even if you did just have an argument). Their minds seem one-tracked when it comes to sex. They do not consider what happened moments before or what will happen later. They also do not consider what else might be going on at the same time. They are difficult to distract. The fact that the kids are awake and running around the house unsupervised means very little once they have zoned in on the target.

Now, don't get me wrong. This creature I have just described is not some kind of an animal (although he may act like it at times); he is your husband. He is not a force to be reckoned with or a beast to be tamed. He is the man you love, and making love to you is essential to his life and the way he views himself and the marriage.

As a loving wife, you need to identify the differences that exist between you and your husband and then evaluate how you can best meet his needs. If we truly understand that sex is a need for our husbands, we will be more willing and able to move toward meeting that need. For men, sex really is more than a recreational activity. Sexual performance is tied directly to self-image. Experiencing a healthy sexual relationship builds confidence as a man and husband. Without this, feelings of insecurity may grow. And he may already be struggling with how he feels about himself and how important he is to you when he sees you taking better care of the kids' needs than his. So as a loving wife, be sure your husband's need to connect with you sexually remains one of your top priorities.

Affection—the Air that She Breathes

Okay, men, now it is your turn. How can you ever understand this creature called woman? Why is she so different from you? Was this God's little joke? Create man with an insatiable need for something that his partner seems never to want anything to do with? No, I don't think so. Although she is very different from you, true intimacy grows in the understanding and acceptance of these differences.

Let's look at it this way. For women, sex is much like having a nice, rich piece of chocolate cake. It is one of those little *luxuries* of life that we allow ourselves to indulge in periodically. It seems to fit best at the end of a full-course meal of conversation, affection, safe touch, and quality time together. It is a perfect ending to a perfect meal. As a matter of fact, we like to take our time with this experience, to savor every bite and truly enjoy its rich and satisfying nature. And once we have indulged, we are satisfied for a while. We usually do not want another piece right away or maybe even for several days. We are content to savor the memory of the last piece of cake and how wonderful it was.

Get the picture? It is not that she does not enjoy sex; most women actually do. It is simply that she does not *require* it the way you do. For her, the cake is the foreplay with intercourse as the icing (so to speak) of the relationship. Icing is not much good without the cake to put it on. On the other hand, even cake without icing is often very enjoyable. So how do you get to the icing? Take time to fix the full-course meal and bake the cake, and I am sure she will be more than happy to ice it for you.

Men, here are some basic concepts to help you better understand this woman God gave you. Your wife is turned on not by your naked body as much as by your conversation. She is aroused by the affection (nonsexual touch and acts of kindness) that you show her throughout the day. For her, arousal is most likely a result of the events of the past several hours or days and not just the here and now. However, the here and now is also important because she can be easily distracted during the process (especially by children running down the hall).

The key concept for women is affection. The presence of affection is absolutely essential for her to experience a satisfying sexual relationship. Affection refers to acts of kindness and love. These acts are not sexual in nature. Rather, they are given solely for the purpose of expressing caring and closeness. Acts of affection include things like holding hands, hugs, cards, flowers, notes left to be found later, winks, opening doors, and many more.

In her mind, affection symbolizes the things she needs most. These include security, comfort, approval, bonding, and protection. The simple act of giving a hug can say so much to her. Such acts of affection say "I love you," "I'm proud of you," "I think you're wonderful," or, "I'm sorry you're hurting." All of these make up the air that she breathes and are essential to the life of her marriage. If affection is absent, women feel insecure, distant, and unloved, and the marriage is at risk. When your wife is missing what is, to her, an essential element of the relationship, her security, self-esteem, and general satisfaction will decrease. She needs to feel close to you, especially through the parenting years. So even when she is too tired for sex, remember you can still feel close and connected through acts of affection and nonsexual touch.

Now that you have a better understanding of your differences, it is time to start working out some ways for the two of you to keep your physical intimacy enjoyable and growing through the hectic years of parenting.

How to Continue Your Sexual Relationship While Parenting

1. Get some rest! It is difficult to get in "the mood" when you can barely hold your eyes open. It is hard to feel sexy when you are sleepy. Take some time to get some sleep. Allow yourself to take a nap during the day when the kids are napping, or take turns sleeping in on Saturday mornings. When you are more rested, you will be more open for a sexual encounter.

2. Make sex an all-day affair. I heard it said somewhere that in the world of sex, men are microwave ovens and women are crockpots. Wow, what a picture. For women, the meal of physical intimacy is all day in the preparing. Making love to her begins with a tender kiss to wake her, winking at her over your first cup of coffee, and calling her from work to tell her you miss her. Then it continues through helping her with dinner and getting the kids to bed, and taking time to snuggle during your favorite television program. Once in bed, you take time to touch, touch, and touch some more. Foreplay is more than a means to an end. Especially for women, foreplay is an end in itself. Her skin is one of her most powerful sexual organs—caress it often. Although this may not be a husband's natural tendency, he will quickly learn that he enjoys the slow-cooked meal more than the microwave kind and will choose it often.

3. Seize the moment. Take time when there is time. Although we all know our time is limited, there is time if you look for it. You have a choice as to how you are going to spend your time when the baby goes down for a nap, or when the kids are watching a video or playing at a neighbor's house. You can focus on household chores or each other. Realizing that private time together is much more important than clean dishes will help you to seize the moments that are available throughout your week.

4. Schedule the time for sex. This helps when the moments just aren't there to "seize." With busy schedules, constant responsibilities, and kids running around, it is easy to lose track of our need to connect physically. We need to remember the importance of sexual intimacy in our relationship and be willing to make time for it. Don't hesitate to pencil in private time with your spouse on your calendar, or take a weekend away to a hotel for privacy.

5. Affirm, appreciate, and adore. There is no limit to the power of words. If you want to draw closer physically and any other way, learn how to build each other up emotionally. Taking time to appreciate, compliment, and generally show that you totally adore your spouse will bring your sweetheart closer than ever.

6. Reach out and touch often. Physical intimacy includes anything the two of you do physically that draws you closer together. When you know there's no time for sex, or when one or both of you simply does not have the energy, you still need to feel close. You can do this by taking time to touch. This may be cuddling on the couch to watch television, holding hands in the car, patting your spouse on the back as you walk by, or kissing before you leave for work. The more you connect in a "safe," nonsexual manner, the closer the two of you will feel.

7. Remember romance before, during, and after. Making love is much more than the act of intercourse and can be enhanced by improving your ability to be romantic in everything you do. Sex improves when you feel close and connected to each other. Romance can make that happen. Make romance a part of every day even when sex is not in the plans, and when sex is in the plans, it will be better than ever. Take time to do little things throughout the day that say I love you, such as love notes, "sweet nothings," and "little somethings"—flowers, moonlight walks, a cup of coffee in bed—and general acts of kindness that say, "I'm thinking of you." When lovemaking is in the plans, work to create a quiet, slow, soft, and relaxed environment. As you do this, you will find that your internal mood begins to match that. You will be better able to push aside the outside world and stress of the day, and slow down and enjoy your time together. Never forget the power of clean sheets, a candlelit room, and soft music.

8. Take care of yourself physically. Do your best to look your best. This means more than just staying in shape or losing that extra ten or twenty pounds (although that is part of it). It also means dressing nicely (even if you are just staying home for the evening). Just how sexy can old, holey sweats, nursing bras, ponytails, or grease-covered jeans really be? Take time to clean up before presenting yourself to your spouse. Take a shower and freshen up. Do your hair and makeup, or shave and clean your fingernails. Do whatever it takes to look the best you can look.

9. Be creative. Avoid getting stuck in a sexual rut. Even if you have to schedule your intimate time together, it does not have to be boring. Scheduling your lovemaking allows each of you to anticipate your time together. Use the time building up to sex to increase your excitement and to plan the activities. Focus on variety in time of day, place, position, setting, and so forth. Keep it interesting and exciting.

10. Be honest—with both your mouth and your body. Communication in any and all forms should be based on honesty. Sex is a form of physical communication. Commit yourselves to honesty with your bodies. Don't fake interest, arousal, enjoyment, or orgasm. If you are not in the mood, or if something does not feel comfortable, talk about it. Dishonesty in the bedroom is just as destructive to the foundation of your relationship as lying with words.

Coming Up Next ...

We have just completed part 1. Hopefully as you have been reading about the nine essential elements to a growing marriage, you already have been applying these to your life. In part 2 we will break down the "Game of the Century" into its distinctive quarters. But even before that, let's take a look at your preseason training. This is the time in your marriage (before children) where you really get to know each other.

PART TWO

THE STAGES
OF MARRIAGE

CHAPTER TEN

AND THE
TWO SHALL
BECOME ONE

Preseason Training: From Wedding to First Pregnancy

*J*im and I met when I was fifteen and he was sixteen—well, that's when he finally noticed me. I had had my eye on him for almost two years before that. We dated all through high school, with only a couple of short-lived breakups. These seemed to be our way of making sure the grass really was not greener on the other side (and of course it wasn't). By the time I graduated from high school, just one year behind Jim, we knew we loved each other and planned to spend the rest of our lives together. Some of our friends who were also high school sweethearts made plans to marry right after graduation. That sounded like a great idea to me. But Jim, being the practical man that he is, knew he was not ready to support a family. He also knew that we both wanted college degrees, and that likely wouldn't happen if we married right then. Someone would have to work to pay bills. Although I was determined that we could just live on love, some part of me knew he was right. We both continued to live at home while we attended a local college and completed our degrees.

Some of our friends teased us that we were going to date forever—and looking back on it, I guess that is what we have tried to do, date forever. This extended dating season of our relationship was a time when we really got to know each other. We talked for hours about everything we could think of. By the time we became officially engaged during my junior year of college, we thought we had totally figured out the world and each other. We each knew how the other thought; we were convinced we could read each other's minds because we were so close. This marriage thing was going to be a cinch. Although some of our friends who had gotten married right after high school were telling us how hard married life was and how unhappy they were, we were convinced that they just had not gotten to know each other the way we had. They had dated for only a year or two, and besides, they were so young. We were much more mature, informed, knowledgeable of each other, and better prepared than any of them. How much more could there be to learn about each other after more than six years of dating? We were ready!

In June 1987, right after graduation from college and just before I was to begin graduate school three and a half hours away, we tied the knot. We were so ready for marital bliss and so sure we were prepared for it that what came next was a rude awakening from a wonderful dream. The couple who was so confident that we had it all together and knew each other so well soon found out that even six years of dating was not enough to stop the explosion that occurs when two lives come crashing into one.

Now, don't get me wrong; parts of that explosion were bursts of complete joy and exhilaration. All of our preparation had not even prepared us for how good the good would be. But that was not the most disturbing part. The most shocking part came when I realized that this man who had spent the previous six years portraying himself as such an intelligent human being was really nothing more than an imposter. What intelligence he did have certainly did not make its way into the bathroom of our little apartment. Not only did he not have the slightest clue where the lid to the toilet belonged, even worse, he held absolutely no understanding of the correct way to place the toilet paper on the roller. I was appalled! How could he have fooled me for six years? How could I, an obviously superior intellectual being, not have noticed the signs of such disabilities? This was just the beginning of our rude awakening. Over the next few months we began to learn things about each other that we simply could never have known until we were married and living together.

"My Side!"

One of our first battles came just after we returned from our honeymoon. We had moved into a small apartment in our hometown in Missouri for a couple of months before our big move to Oklahoma. The back door of this apartment happened to be in the one and only bedroom (this will be important in a minute). Although I thought this odd, I did not see it as any big deal.

It was our first night home, and we were getting ready for bed. I was finishing washing my face when I heard Jim jump into bed. As I anticipated curling up beside him to snuggle, I came around the corner and into the bedroom, only to see him lying *on my side of the bed! Okay, maybe this is a joke,* I thought and started playfully telling him to get on his side of the bed. He laughed and said, "I am on my side of the bed. Now, come here."

Still thinking he was just being playful, I decided to tickle him from "my side," hoping he would move away at least far enough for me to squeeze in. But he didn't. Within a few minutes, we both realized that the other was not joking and this was about to become a real issue between us. I was quickly playing back the first week of marriage in my mind. Why had this not become an issue before tonight? All I could determine was that it had been our honeymoon, and I guess who was where in the bed had not been high on our priority list.

So there we were, about to lock horns in a battle to the death over "my side" of the bed. I know this may sound funny now, but believe me, it was no laughing matter. The next several minutes were spent with each of us presenting our arguments, reasons, excuses, and bribes, but no one was budging. We were both convinced we could sleep only on that particular side of the bed, and we were at a deadlock. That is, until Jim went silent for just a moment. (Can't you just see the wheels turning? I could.) Then he said what turned out to be the determining factor for where we still sleep to this day. He said, "Debbie, don't you believe that it's my job as your husband to protect you? That's all I want to do. You are my wife and I want to keep you safe. The back door is right next to our bed. I need to sleep on this side so I can be between you and anyone who might come through that door."

That settled it. My big, strong, highly intelligent husband simply wanted to protect me. Is that sweet or what? And as I crawled into the other side of the bed, I felt more in love than ever. Wow, this marriage thing is great.

And now for "The Rest of the Story." Two months later we moved to Oklahoma, into a tiny house that was not arranged at all like our little apartment and had no back door in our bedroom. The door it did have happened to be on what I still thought of as rightfully "my side" of the bed. I saw this as a gift from God for my being so good and submitting two months before and allowing Jim to "protect" me. I was about to return to my rightful place and "my side."

That night, Jim was lying on "my side" again! What was this? He probably just did that out of habit. So I lovingly asked him, didn't he want to move to the other side where the door is, so he could protect me? He looked at me like I was crazy. "What are you talking about?" was all he said. I reminded him of what he had said back in our apartment, and I saw a smile start to move across his face. He admitted to having said that just so he could have that side of the bed and added that there was no sense in moving now as I was probably already used to the other side. I was floored. I had been completely outsmarted. Now who was the "superior intellectual being"?

Our first few months (maybe years) were full of learning new things about each other. Some were pleasant; others were not. Like the night I woke up to a loud yell from the bathroom and a husband limping back into our bedroom trying not to cry. That was the night he learned that I am not too good at closing drawers. Or the first (and unfortunately not the last) time Jim learned that the checkbook and I are great friends, but keeping a running balance is not part of that friendship. I have definitely learned the hard way that having checks does not mean you have money. Or the day he realized I was not joking when I said I could not cook. All of these were just part of our growing experiences.

Time to Leave and Cleave

One of the hardest adjustments either of us experienced came about two months into our marriage. We were moving away from our hometown so I could attend graduate school. You would have thought this would have been an exciting time for us. We were about to be free from our families to live our own life, make our own way, blaze our own path. But no matter how many times I told myself that, it just never really soaked in. This period was probably the most difficult for Jim. The problem was not that he had a hard time with the move; it was that he could not have been prepared for the meltdown his wife was about to have.

From the moment we drove out of Carthage, Missouri, and for

the next three months solid, Jim had to adjust to a wife who cried at least once a day. Now, this was not just your normal, wimpy, drop-a-tear-or-two kind of crying. No, this was the full-blown, two-fisted tissue, hyperventilating, "I want to go home!" kind of crying. How dare he take me away from my family and move me three and a half hours away! (Of course, I was not rational enough to consider that we moved for *me* to go to school.) All I could think about was how far away my family was and why wasn't he taking me home. At times, he would ask me if I hated being married. I know now he was wondering if I thought I had made a mistake in marrying him. But that was not it at all. I didn't want to be away from him! I loved him! I just did not want to be away from my family, either. I wanted both of us to go back home. Once Jim realized that, he was great and did his very best to get me home practically every weekend for those first three months. Thank goodness he was patient, and eventually I realized that "home" is wherever he is.

The early years of marriage can be just as stressful and difficult as the later years, but for different reasons. Although you may not be adjusting to a new screaming baby or trying to parent a rebellious teen, you are trying to do one of the most difficult tasks of all time: become one flesh.

Blending two people with different backgrounds, learning experiences, family histories, and expectations into one marriage is nothing short of a miracle. Maybe that is why God must be in the center of it to really make it work. But even with God right smack dab in the middle of the two of you, there will be clashes, changes, concessions, and compromises. That is what this "preseason" training stage of the marriage is for—to spend time developing a strong connection between the two of you and to start learning and applying the skills that will become the foundation of a strong marriage that can really go the distance. It is about learning to "leave and cleave" and becoming one flesh.

Preseason Training

Any good sports team that hopes to be the best will spend time together during the preseason. What for? To become a better team. They use preseason training to learn new plays, grow in their understanding of one another's strengths and weaknesses, determine who plays what position, build each other up, and work out their differences. The more of this that they can accomplish before the actual games begin, the more likely it is that the team will reach its goal of being a winning team.

The same is true for the marital team. They must learn about each other, develop a set of skills for the upcoming game, and grow in their understanding of each other's needs and of each other's strengths and weaknesses. They must determine and negotiate marital roles, discuss expectations, and learn to build each other up.

All of these skills are what you need to focus on during those early years of marriage before the children arrive. One of the main tasks during this stage is learning how to meet the emotional and physical needs of your spouse. This involves learning about marital roles as well as the skills necessary to understand how your spouse experiences love. No matter how long you dated, you will have to make adjustments and transitions in this phase of your relationship. Communication skills will be tested and developed as you work to solve day-to-day problems and differences and as you start to experience unmet needs and expectations. Learning to think in terms of "we" instead of "I" can also be difficult, especially with so many adults waiting longer and longer to marry, thus having more single "I" time to overcome.

You are doing more than becoming husband and wife. You are in the process of joining two entirely separate families through each of your personal experiences, beliefs, and upbringings. There are some basic things that need to be addressed and worked on in this stage of marriage that will go a long way toward developing a marriage that will last "until death do us part."

Expectations

This stage is a good time to identify your family differences and your personal expectations of marriage that result from your unique upbringing. (You may want to review chapter 2.) We all have expectations, even if we are not aware of them. Most of our expectations are not voiced—or even recognized—until they have been broken. When a spouse does not do or say something that we "expected," we realize it and react—often not too positively. There is no way you will be able to identify every expectation or discuss every situation you may face and consider how you would want to deal with it. However, the process of learning to identify and discuss expectations as you realize them creates a healthy building block for discussions when stressful situations arise in the future.

During this stage of your relationship, discussions regarding expectations may be about general marital issues such as how often the house should be cleaned and by whom, whether to have joint or separate checking accounts, and who sleeps on which side of the bed. You may also discuss expectations about future stages, such as children and parenting. You may have discussed expectations, hopes, and desires about some of these issues before you were married, but you will need to address them again at this stage. Here is a list of just a few questions that may help to get you started talking about your expectations:

1. Do we want to have children? If so, when, how many, and how close together?
2. How do we think children will change our relationship?
3. Will we both continue to work outside the home?

4. If we cannot get pregnant, would we consider adoption? Fertility testing?
5. If we both continue our careers, how will we manage sick kids?
6. What do we expect each other's roles to be in raising our children?
7. How will our division of labor within the home change when we have children?

Healthy Communication

Taking time to develop the healthiest communication skills you can at this stage can save you much heartache in future stages that are even more stressful. Couples are often very good at both talking and listening during dating. This open and honest sharing is how you became so close and what made you feel you knew each other so well. You took time to really listen to each other and gave each other your undivided attention on a regular basis.

Once married, these skills (like many of the healthy skills of dating) seem to get lost in the shuffle of daily events. The time you have available is less and less as the children arrive. So take advantage of the fact that during this stage there is more time for the two of you to communicate and grow closer. Use the time available in this stage to develop the best communication habits possible, which will help you make it through to that last stage, when once again you will find that you have more time for each other. Take time to develop a habit of talking to each other daily, even if only for fifteen to twenty minutes. Turn the television off and share with each other about your day or any other topic that is of interest. Without strong communication skills, the other stages could end up driving the two of you apart. Be sure to learn how to handle conflict in a way that actually resolves the issue and does not just sweep it under the rug, only to have it rear its ugly head in the future.

Treasuring Each Other

We each experience love in different ways. Part of your job in these early years of marriage is to be a student of your spouse. Learn everything you can about him or her, and put into action what you learn. Finding out how you can make your spouse feel loved is essential to experiencing continued closeness. Staying close also requires that you continue to do the things you did during dating and courtship that drew you close together in the first place. If you want to stay in love forever, commit to doing the things that made you fall in love in the first place—and do them forever. I am told that you should not repeat things when writing, but I feel this is worth repeating: *If you want to stay in love forever, commit to doing the things that made you fall in love in the first place—and do them forever!*

Ten Steps to Growing Stronger through this Stage

1. Communicate daily. Talk, talk, talk, and talk some more. Take time to communicate about both big and little things. Practice sharing at levels three through five (see chapter 6), because the better you get at these skills, the stronger you will be through the rest of the stages. It will be especially helpful to refine the skills of FAIR fighting so you will know how to resolve conflicts (see chapter 7).

2. Define what your relationship is going to look like. Remember that each of you has a unique history and experiences that have formed your way of thinking. Be open to seeing things from a new perspective, and work hard to avoid the trap of "I've never done it that way before." Flexibility is the key and works best if you remember that "different" does not mean "wrong."

3. Be patient with each other. You are each learning a whole new set of roles and skills, and this learning process is going to take some time. Moving from the "me" mindset to the "we" mindset can be difficult, and the longer you were single and independent, the longer this adjustment may take. Focus on each other's positive characteristics and efforts, and avoid criticizing the negatives.

4. Develop the habit of "treasuring" your spouse. To develop a habit, you repeat a behavior over and over for an extended period. When we think of habits, we often think of the bad habits we have developed. But if we work at it, we can develop healthy habits in relationships as well. Spending positive time together on a regular basis and learning how your spouse experiences love from you are two of the best habits you can create to keep a marriage going strong for years to come.

5. Find the appropriate balance. Reaching a balance between couple time, friend time, and self time will help keep the two of you closer in the long run. Time is a precious commodity and always seems to be in short supply. Although this stage of your relationship may feel harried, "Baby, you ain't seen nothing yet!" The time you have available to do with as you choose will increasingly become virtually extinct. Learning now to set aside time for your relationship, your friends, and yourself will help you remember to do this even after the children arrive.

6. Have a date at least once a week. I cannot emphasize this enough. Most couples took special time out of their schedules for alone time with each other (that is called a date) before the wedding, but seem to think it is not necessary once they are married. The need for special time together never ends, and simply living in the same house does not count. You may have to learn the art of creative dating once you are married because money may be in short supply. So get creative about things you can do together that do not cost much. Take a walk hand in hand, go on a picnic, check out a movie from the library, or do a jigsaw puzzle together. The possibilities are endless once you start brainstorming.

7. Pray for each other and with each other. Building spiritual intimacy can be difficult for some couples. This may be a result of never seeing it demonstrated in their childhood homes or because of past church experiences. Talk about your desire to keep God at the center of your marriage, and commit to praying for each other daily. Share specific areas that you struggle with, and ask your spouse to pray for those needs. Praying out loud with each other is a precious bonding time once you each get past any anxiety that you may have. Start out slowly, maybe by taking turns praying at meal times or before bed for just a few minutes. You will soon see that your time together in prayer will grow, and you will feel closer than ever.

8. Take time to resolve personal issues. If you did not do this before you got married, be sure to take time now. Your relationship and future family will all benefit from your being as healthy personally as you can possibly be. As you evaluate who you are, where you came from, how you view the world and who you want to be, you will become aware of possible problem areas in your life. Identifying these areas and working to resolve any unresolved personal baggage from your past will help destroy future barriers to intimacy.

9. Enjoy each other physically. The physical aspect of your relationship is not going to just develop on its own. It takes time and communication to make physical intimacy the most satisfying it can be for the two of you. Use this time without children for the two of you to experiment sexually and find out what you like and what you do not. Share your expectations, needs, hopes, and desires for this area of your relationship. Remember to take time to touch often in both sexual and nonsexual ways. Don't let the practice of holding hands, hugging, and kissing get lost or be replaced by sex. Both aspects of your physical relationship are important and actually will feed off each other.

10. Commit to each other for the long haul. Openly communicate in both words and actions that you are here for better or worse. Commit to each other that you will not run away or escape when the going gets tough. No one runs home to mommy, walks out on a fight, or stops communicating. Security in a relationship grows when you commit to staying there and working through the hard times.

Coming Up Next ...

The preseason is over and the real game is about to begin. No matter how much practice you have had, the next few years of your life will challenge you at a whole new level. The birth of your first child can be one of the most exhilarating times of your life. However, if you are not prepared for the inevitable changes that will come to your relationship, you may be in for some rough waters ahead. Turn the page and start learning how to keep your marriage relationship as a top priority even in the presence of those little "time thieves" we call babies. Let the game begin!

CHAPTER ELEVEN

WHEN ONE PLUS ONE EQUALS THREE

First Quarter: From Infancy through Preschool

reseason training comes screeching to a halt when a little blue line or plus sign announces that the "Game of the Century" is about to begin in your home. Regardless of how long you have been training, it is now time to put those skills to the test. And what a test it will be! It is one thing to run these drills with your teammate. It is a different experience when you realize you have a formidable opponent who does not give up or give in. This little creature will throw at you everything possible that just might cause your team to break down.

You soon realize that you had completely underestimated your opponent based on size and intellectual development. This tiny wonder is actually more powerful than dynamite and has the unspoken capability to rock your entire world. Every skill you have practiced will be tested to the limit, and you will find yourselves having to develop new and stronger tactics as the game progresses. Does this seem extreme? After all, we are only talking about a baby, right? Wrong! What we are talking about is a radical change in what you have come to know as your marriage. This tiny bundle has the ability to bring both boundless joy and immeasurable stress. The transition into parenthood will bring new feelings of uncertainty and insecurity as you quickly learn that you are no longer the one in control. Life as you once knew it will never be the same again.

Trying to Be Perfect

Angela and Rob had been married for just over three years and felt their relationship was stronger than ever. They had had a pretty rough first year. Not only did they experience the normal "getting to really know each other" issues that every couple faces, they also grieved the loss of Rob's dad just a few weeks after their wedding. Later that same year, Rob's company downsized and he found himself without a job and only two weeks' pay. Both Rob and Angela wondered how they would ever survive all the conflicts, stress, and financial pressure. But somehow, they did. By the time they had weathered these major storms of life, they found themselves closer than ever and felt sure that they could tackle anything the world might throw at them. That was until the world decided to throw a seven-pound bombshell into their home.

Emma's arrival was met with joy and excitement. They had both wanted to have children and were ecstatic when they found out Angela was pregnant. They spent the next several months doing all the things expecting parents do. They read all the how-to books, planned and prepared the nursery, argued over names, and talked about how fun this was going to be. The only down point either of them seemed to experience was the feelings of sadness that

Rob's dad wouldn't be there to see his first grandchild and that the baby would never know her granddad. That wound was still tender, and the birth of a baby seemed to make it more obvious. But they supported each other as they shared their grief and were still sure this was going to be the best thing ever to happen to them.

Angela delivered Emma naturally and without complications; only later did she realize that she had considered this a feather in her cap and one more indication that she was going to be able to handle anything. Nothing could be worse than the pain she had endured through twenty-one hours of labor and delivery. If she could manage that, she was sure this parenting thing was going to be a cinch. But within a couple of days, she realized how wrong she was.

Although Emma looked like the perfect baby, she was anything but perfect. She cried all the time, slept little, wanted to eat constantly, yet would not latch on appropriately when Angela attempted to breastfeed (which, of course, was the "perfect" way to feed your baby). The vicious cycle of Emma not getting enough to eat, then not sleeping long enough, then waking up crying and wanting to eat again but not getting enough was beginning to make Angela feel as though she was not being the perfect parent. What could she be doing wrong? Why was this baby so unhappy?

Angela kept pushing herself and her baby harder to "get this thing right." But as time progressed, both mother and baby became more tired, irritable, and cranky. Nothing was working, and Angela was faced with what she called her first "failure" as a mom just two weeks after Emma was born. At the baby's two-week checkup, the doctor determined that Emma was not growing sufficiently. She was still significantly below her birth weight, and the doctor told Angela she needed to start supplementing breastfeeding with formula. This sent shock waves through Angela, and all she could hear in her head was, "You're not good enough," and, "You can't do anything right."

Rob attempted to assure her that she was doing a great job and that no one expected her to breastfeed. Secretly he was even a little glad Emma would be taking a bottle because that meant he could be more involved. He had not shared his feelings with Angela, but he was beginning to feel a little left out of this whole parenting thing. It seemed as though every time he wanted to hold and play with the baby, Angela (or Emma) would inform him that it was time for Emma to eat and off they would go. Angela would complain about being tired and exhausted, but she was not really allowing Rob to step in and help. He saw bottle feeding as a great opportunity for him to play a more active role and also to give Angela some much-needed rest. But when he said that to Angela, he was met with another wave of tears. "You don't think I can do this either, do you?" No amount of assurance seemed to make Angela feel better. But she knew she had to do what was best for the baby, so she purchased the bottles and formula.

The next few weeks seemed to get worse, not better. Although Rob was attending to the baby much more than before and was even getting up to do the three AM feeding, he was not enjoying this. Why? Because Angela would not just let him do it. If she was not standing directly over him giving "suggestions" about how to hold the bottle or when to stop and burp Emma, then she was asking him how much Emma had eaten or if he had warmed the bottle. He felt constantly criticized, and he resented that Angela was not taking advantage of his help and getting more rest. It seemed to him that if Angela was not doing it, it was not being done right.

By this time, they were both sleep-deprived, insecure, and irritable and were beginning to take it out on each other. The arguments between them increased and did not focus only on issues about Emma. They seemed to be able to fight about just about anything. Before long, they found themselves just going through the motions of the day, doing what had to be done and interacting as little as possible. Until one day Rob came home from work to find both mother and baby in tears. What was wrong?

"I just can't take this anymore. I'm a horrible mother and an even worse wife. I can't seem to do anything right or make either one of you happy. I just want my old life back. Why didn't someone tell me how bad this was going to be?" Angela continued to cry and Rob's heart was breaking. What had happened to them? They had survived a horrible first year and now were seemingly being destroyed by an innocent baby. This had to stop. They had to regain their life.

Rob got the baby to sleep, and then he and Angela spent the next couple of hours trying to figure out what was going wrong. They realized that they were going to need some outside help to get through this. They loved each other enough to seek counseling. About a week later, the two of them sat in my office, with Emma in tow, and described what had been happening in their relationship. We spent the next several weeks discussing the things that will be presented in this chapter and helping them begin to reclaim their marriage while accepting the struggles of parenting.

Coping with Change

What's really going to change? I can answer that question in one word: everything! And the changes start as soon as you either decide you are ready to have children or find out that you are pregnant. Your communication skills will be put to the test in this stage and will prove essential in your adjustment and continued feelings of closeness and satisfaction. Not only will you have brand-new things to discuss, but you will also have more conflicts to resolve. Working together to openly discuss changing needs, emotional reactions, and newly identified expectations will help reduce the conflicts that will likely arise if these things are not discussed.

This stage of marriage holds so many changes and adjustments that there are several unique topics to talk about. One of these is related to the issues of pregnancy and the changes this brings. Couples in this early stage of parenting face anxieties about pregnancy and childbirth. Many a mom expresses concerns about how she looks physically, the pain of labor, and the health of the unborn baby. A dad, on the other hand, may spend the pregnancy months worrying about his wife's health, the possibility of her death during childbirth, how their sexual relationship will change, and being able to provide financially for his new family.

Sharing these fears and concerns openly with your spouse can help you feel less alone with your thoughts and closer to your spouse. Give each other support and validate the other's feelings even if you do not completely understand them. Avoid attempting to make them feel better by telling them, "That's not going to happen," or other such responses. That kind of response tends to make the other person feel negated and less likely to share in the future. So be supportive and keep talking.

Once the baby arrives, you may ask, "Whatever happened to sleeping in, spontaneity, late-night movies, and holding hands?" Baby happened, that's what. No matter how much you each wanted this new little bundle of joy, you need to be prepared for rough waters ahead. The changes that occur at the birth of your first child are immeasurable, and at some point you will realize that life will never be the same again. This stage includes an emotional roller coaster such as you could never have imagined. You go from the joy of seeing your new creation for the first time to the fear of being inadequate as a parent, from the pride of watching your child develop and learn each new skill to the loneliness of feeling disconnected from your spouse. And on and on the roller coaster goes.

This new stage of your relationship requires that you change certain expectations of how much energy you will have at the end of the day for conversation or housework. How you define closeness and intimacy may need to be changed as well. Be aware of changes in your personal emotional needs. Mom often begins to develop an emotional need for family commitment that was not there before. She may need to see her husband actively participating in the parenting and will feel close to him as she watches him in his role as a father.

On the other hand, dad often develops an increased need to feel he is providing adequately for his new family. The responsibilities of finances and job may increase his need for admiration from his wife for the role he is performing. As these emotional needs change, it is essential that you identify them within yourself and then talk to your spouse. I have yet to meet the spouse who is a flawless mind reader; so if you want your spouse to know that your needs are changing, then say so.

The new stresses that flood into new parents' lives seem unending. You are now dealing with identifying your new roles as mom and dad when you most likely had barely gotten the hang of being husband and wife. You are also learning the new skills of infant care and parenting and are physically drained by the never-ending need for attention from your little one. All this is mixed with increased conflicts with your spouse over role responsibilities, lack of emotional and physical support, and changes in your sexual relationship. Top that all off with increased financial demands, and you have the perfect formula for a major drop in marital satisfaction. Actually, research shows that there is a significant drop in perceived marital satisfaction and an increase in marital conflicts after the birth of the first child. This drop in satisfaction is usually greater for the wife and is still present at the end of the first year.[1] Why might this be?

Two Major Threats to Marriage

There are two major threats to the marital bond, and they begin here, in the first quarter of parenting. What are they? Lack of time and lack of energy. The feelings of grief at a loss of couple time, feelings of disconnectedness from your spouse, feelings of jealously about the amount of time and attention baby is receiving, and the loss of energy all cause a great shift in the intimacy pattern. If the couple does not recognize these threats and deal with them openly, they may begin to feel even more alone and isolated from each other.

The Changing Pace of Time

In our counseling sessions, Angela shared that her perception of time seemed to have changed since Emma was born. Trying to keep to a feeding and sleeping schedule made her constantly aware of the clock. "I think I've looked at the clock more in the last six weeks than ever in my life. I'm constantly calculating how long it has been since Emma's last feeding or how long until the next. The more I look at the clock, the faster time seems to fly."

There is some truth in Angela's perceptions. The most changed aspect of the new parents' lives is the aspect of time. The time available for sleeping, eating, watching television, talking, sex, and even bathroom time seems to have just disappeared. Eating and napping schedules make parents more aware than ever of the clock. This constant awareness tends to make the new parents feel as though time is always running out. You can no longer take things for granted, and what used to come easily now takes more effort than you feel able to give.

Not only is a couple's perception of time changing, but the actual amount of time that they can choose what to do with decreases tremendously. A couple will have only about one-third as much discretionary time after the baby is born as they had before their first child.[2] With the overwhelming demands of caring for a new baby added to all the requirements of daily living already present, something is going to have to give. And unfortunately, that "something" is usually the marriage, and more specifically—the spouse. After all, isn't he or she big enough to take care of himself or herself? It is easy to let the other supposedly independent adult in the house take a backseat to the crying baby and just about everything else. The dishes are not going to wash themselves, and the laundry isn't going to fold itself, but we convince ourselves that the marriage is going to grow itself. Of course, this is not true. We must work on reestablishing priorities to make sure that the marital relationship ranks higher than dirty diapers and dishes.

Here are a few suggestions to help try to make the most of the time you do have available:

1. Be selective about what outside commitments you make. Be willing to say no to friends, family, work events, and so forth. Your time as a couple is so limited that you must first take into account the amount of time the two of you have together before planning outside engagements. Avoid overcommitting, and set priorities for your time. There are only so many hours in a day or week. You cannot expect to keep doing everything you have always done once you start adding children to the list of daily requirements.

2. Take advantage of nap time or early morning time. While the baby is still asleep, enjoy a cup of coffee together and chat about your day. You may want to read the paper together and share your thoughts or simply hold hands and snuggle while you watch the news or a favorite television program.

3. Turn the television off. Television is not evil, but if not limited, it can eat up a lot of precious time. If you are in the habit of having the television on even when you have no intention of watching it, you probably have realized how easy it is to get drawn into something that you would never have chosen to watch. Plan ahead by being selective about which television programs you want to watch. When the program is over, turn the television set off. Many couples in recent years have decided to cut television out of their lives altogether, or at least cut down to a select few hours a week. Jim and I made this decision shortly after the birth of our first child. Up until then, I would say we were both "TVaholics." But once Taffeta arrived, we realized we would much rather spend our time enjoying her and each other. We also realized our responsibility to protect our child from negative influences that are portrayed on some shows. The television disappeared (well, except for *Monday Night Football*—that's a must). We have really not missed it, and now with three children in the home I have a hard time understanding how anyone could spend hours in front of the television and still get everything done.

The second of the two most deadly threats to marital stability and satisfaction has to do with the lack of energy you have available to devote to your relationship. You feel as though you are constantly running on empty during the first few months (and sometimes years) of parenting. Sleep deprivation is a given for any couple with a baby in the house, and it is one of the biggest culprits in stealing our energy.

Annie came into my office as a mother of two young children (four months and two years) who felt she was about to have a "breakdown." When I asked her about this, she said she was seriously considering admitting herself to a hospital just so she could get some rest. Then she burst into tears. She described feeling as though she had not had a solid night of sleep in almost two years. Even when her husband "took the night shift" at home with the kids, she still did not feel rested. All she wanted to do was go away somewhere and sleep for a week.

She described a "normal" day like this:

"I get up by six so I can get a shower before my husband leaves for work; otherwise, I will never get one. If I'm lucky, I can clean up the kitchen from the night before or throw in a load of laundry before the baby wakes up. The morning is filled with feeding the baby, fixing breakfast for Tiffany, getting everyone dressed, and trying to make it to either my moms' group, Bible study, or the gym, depending on the day. And sometimes I just don't go because it's just too much effort. All I can think and pray about is hoping both kids will take a nap at the same time so maybe I can sleep, too. But that rarely happens. Usually the baby falls asleep on the car ride home from wherever we've been and then wakes up about the time Tiffany is ready to go to sleep.

"I spend some time in the afternoon playing with Tiffany or reading her books and teaching her some new songs. I try to get a few things done around the house. But between changing diapers, feeding the baby, keeping a two-year-old out of the cabinets, and thinking about fixing dinner, I simply don't get anything done. Brian comes home and, although he doesn't say anything, I'm sure he's disappointed in how the house looks—I would be. He comes in and plays with the girls so I can fix dinner, and then it's bath and bedtime.

"By then all I want to do is collapse into my own bed and sleep. But that's when Brian wants to talk or have sex. He's got to be crazy! Or maybe I am. That's why I'm here."

Over the next few weeks, both Annie and Brian spent time in my office working on rebuilding their relationship and helping Annie get the rest she so desperately needed. This lack of energy and sleep on her part was affecting the entire family and especially their marriage. Brian was feeling desperate for some time with his wife and was beginning to build resentment toward her and even the children. He felt she gave all the energy she had to the kids and her outside activities and saved nothing for him. He was not even getting the leftovers because there seemed to be no leftovers. She was completely drained before he even got home from work. Annie, on the other hand, was feeling drained as soon as she woke up in the morning. It was not that she purposely used up all her energy through the day; it was that she started out empty and spent the day running on vapors to do what she thought "had to be done."

Brian and Annie worked on openly sharing their feelings and needs, and started reprioritizing their lives in such a way as to meet these needs. Brian started by getting Annie a weekend away just for her. She was thrilled to have two nights and three days to do whatever she wanted—which she was sure was going to be just sleep, sleep, and more sleep. Actually, after the first good night's sleep, she took time to get a massage, read a book, and take a long bath. By the end of the weekend, she was feeling revitalized and couldn't wait to see her family. They both knew that sleep would continue to be in short supply, but they could begin to take steps to improve on the energy they had available for each other.

Here are some suggestions to help couples learn to improve their energy and savor what limited energy they do have available:

1. Trade off by giving each other a break from the "night shift" and treating each other with a special "sleep-in" day.

2. Start an exercise program together. Exercising and getting in shape will not only increase your energy level, but doing it together helps the two of you have some couple time.

3. Get away for an overnight stay somewhere as often as possible.

4. Hire someone to help clean the house, prepare meals, or do laundry. Anything you can get someone else to do reserves energy for the two of you for later.

5. Eat out or order pizza at least once a week.

6. Take the kids to Mother's Day Out even when all you plan to do is go home and rest.

7. Choose your individual activities wisely, being sure to reserve energy for your spouse first and foremost.

Ten Steps to Survive and Thrive through the First Quarter

1. Be flexible and do not expect perfection. Remember, everything is changing, and it takes time to adjust and find your way through this new maze of responsibilities and roles. Being flexible, both with yourself and your spouse, will reduce tension. There is no "right" way to parent. You will develop a routine that works for the two of you and your baby. Do not worry if it is not the same as the way some of your friends are doing it. Avoid setting unrealistic expectations for either of you or the baby. Be sure to take time to share with each other if you feel that unrealistic expectations are forming, and then discuss these openly. Be careful not to expect perfection, because if you do not expect it then you will not have to feel pressured to reach for something you can never attain.

2. Find a balance. For now, the needs and demands of your baby will likely take center stage in this three-ring circus you are calling a marriage. But remember, there are two other rings to attend to as well—you and your spouse. Doing little things to take care of your spouse and yourself can make all the difference in the world. While the baby naps, do something for one or both of you instead of focusing on catching up on household chores. For example, take a nap, call a friend, read a magazine, or chat with your spouse.

3. Talk to each other every day. Take time every day to check in with each other. Talk about changing expectations and needs, division of labor, disappointments and fears about parenting, whatever you want—just keep talking. Remember that communication involves both talking and listening. You need to be the best listener you can possibly be if you want your spouse to continue to share with you his or her deepest thoughts, feelings, fears, and needs.

4. Get out of the house. This can be with or without the baby, because both can be fun. Fresh air, fresh faces, and fresh conversation can help you avoid feeling that the world is passing you by. Get out there and be a part of the activities that you and your spouse choose together. This will help contain feelings of loneliness and isolation that many parents of young children experience.

5. Develop a couple-centered, not a child-centered, relationship. This is the first time in your relationship that you have to choose who really comes first. Starting right here and now, determine that the couple comes before the children. The order of priorities must be God first, marriage second, and children third if you want your marriage to continue to grow stronger through each of the consecutive stages. If you make your children your number one or even number two priority, their never-ending need for attention will eat up everything you have to give, and the rest of your life will suffer because of it. Love your children, provide for them, and meet their needs. But remember that one of their most important needs is to have parents who really love each other.

6. Become coparents, not compulsive parents. One of the major problems I see couples having today has to do with the "superparent" role so many of us believe we have to take on. Moms and dads alike (usually moms more than dads at this stage) can fall into the trap of believing they are the only person who can adequately care for the baby. Somehow they forget that many a parent has come and gone before them and has learned to care adequately for these helpless little creatures just as they have. But when it comes to their baby, they are convinced that it has to be done a certain way, and no one can do it as well as they can. This can even apply to the other parent. Becoming a compulsive parent will only isolate you and eventually lead to parenting burnout. Parents need breaks and need to support each other. Work to become coparents, allowing each of you to care for your baby and being flexible in how things are done. If your husband offers to give the baby a bath and starts at the opposite end than you would, so what? The baby is getting clean and you do not have to do it.

7. **Redefine romance.** Let's face it, intimacy and romance as they were once defined become much more difficult once you become a parent. The availability of privacy and time for just the two of you may seem almost nonexistent. And when it is available, you may not have the energy to focus or perform. During this stage of parenting, find new ways to stay connected physically. Be respectful of mom's healing from delivery, each other's energy level and desires for physical intimacy, as well each other's different needs for romance. You may find yourselves touching more often in nonsexual ways and wanting to cuddle up together at night, even though you may not desire anything more. Be patient with each other in this area, and remind each other that "this too shall pass" and you will be able to regain spontaneous, uninterrupted love-making in the future.

8. Establish an outside support network. This includes friends and family you can call on for help on an especially stressful day or who are there as a sounding board and to offer advice. This also includes anyone you can hire to help out with daily chores such as housecleaning, laundry, meal preparation, and lawn mowing. And don't forget those moms' groups, Bible studies, and couples from church that can help fill your need for adult conversation. If someone offers to help out, accept! Don't try to go it alone. Staying connected to the world around you and reserving your energy will greatly help in dealing with the stress and feelings of isolation that many new parents experience.

9. Schedule couple time. Busy couples do not just find time for each other; they make time for each other. Taking time to connect with your spouse every day is an essential element to keeping a marriage strong. Remember to kiss every day, hug each other as you leave and return home, sit together holding hands while you watch television. These little connection times can make all the difference in the world in helping the two of you feel treasured by each other. Set aside a large block of time to spend together at least once a week. Hire a babysitter, get away from the house and baby, and remember who you married and why. You did not get married to have children; you got married because you were in love with each other. Now, while you are raising children, keep reminding each other what it is you love about the other. Spending time together, dating, and talking with each other are the best ways to do this.

10. Develop a sense of humor, because when all else fails (and it probably will at least once in a while), it helps to laugh!

Coming Up Next ...

If you thought this stage was draining, just wait. The second quarter of parenting includes those years when we have early-school-age children. These are highly energetic creatures who seem to have an unending desire to be "doing something." And to top it all off, many of us are crazy enough to believe that two (or three or four) is better than one, and we end up juggling the needs and activities of multiple children. Staying connected to your spouse may be more difficult at this stage than at any other and will take some special skills. Those skills will be the focus of the next chapter.

CHAPTER TWELVE

AND THEY'RE OFF!

Second Quarter: The Early-school-age Years

*J*ust when you think you are beginning to get it all figured out, you realize that you really do not have a clue. This whole parenting thing just seems to keep changing, and now you are smack-dab in the middle of the most physically draining of all the stages. You may be trying to manage more than one child, and if so, your children are likely in different stages of development and need different things from you. You have just hit the "survival zone" of parenting. Although you thought you were prepared to start playing the "Game of the Century," you are now beginning to wonder. The first quarter definitely took its toll on you and seemed as though it would never end. As the second quarter begins, you are already exhausted and have no idea how you can possibly make it to halftime—when you hope for a little rest. For now, you would be happy if someone would call a time-out and give you a chance to come up for air. Overall, you have played well, but as you move into the second quarter, you now have to rally some energy up to make it to halftime.

The Challenge of More Than One

One of the most challenging parts of this stage is that it is often blended with the previous stage. Most of us who choose to have children seem determined not to stop at one. Depending on the spacing of the children, we may move one into school while a little one is still in diapers (or maybe on the way). We seem to think that once we get through the pain, stress, and adjustments of our first-born, we have this whole parenting thing figured out. So why not do it again? I'm here to tell you that having your second child is not like learning to swim. When you learn to swim, you fight to get the skills down just as soon as you possibly can in order to avoid drowning. Once you know the basics of how to tread water, float, and maybe even do a few strokes, you can relax. You can jump right in next time and know what to do. No worries, right? Not so with parenting. No matter how you did with child number one, you will be faced with learning it all over again—and with some new and added twists.

I remember when Tiara arrived three years after Taffeta. We were sure we had this parenting thing down to a science. Boy, were we wrong! Not only because Tiara's temperament and personality were so different from Taffeta's, but because we had never had a new baby with a three-year-old in the house. And this was not just any three-year-old. This was a highly demanding, strong-willed, independent, and jealous little three-year-old. As Jim and I tried to adjust and give both girls the attention they needed, we felt there just was not enough of us to go around. It was not long before we resorted to the "divide and conquer" method of parenting, which simply meant that we spent less time together as a couple and more time chasing our little ones in different directions. When we passed in the hallway, we would smile and say, "I'm just glad there are two of us. Can you imagine trying to handle this alone?" (Believe me, I have a great deal of respect for those single parents out there going it alone.)

Once we finally settled into a routine that seemed to work, and we were getting to see each other once in a while during a family evening, along came Cherry baby number three. We were really sure we had this thing down now, because we had done the "baby-with-a-sibling-at-home" experience. And although the change from one child to two was difficult, we did survive it and with only minimal scars from the battle. *It can't be that much different to add just one more.* We were wrong again! (We were getting good at being wrong—it must be practice for when the kids reach their teen years.)

The adjustment from one child to two was much harder than we thought it was going to be. But it was nothing compared to the move from two children to three. That was exponentially more difficult. There was no more "divide and conquer," at least not on our part. We were now outnumbered, and if anything, the children seemed to have the upper hand and were becoming skilled at dividing and conquering the parents. We struggled to feel we were effective at parenting, and we faltered in our ability to be a good couple. There was so much more to do in raising three children, and each of them seemed to need something completely different. We had a new baby who needed constant care, a three-year-old who had just had to give up her bedroom for this baby she wasn't even sure she liked yet, and a first grader who just wanted to learn to read "harder" books. We were pulled in so many different directions that the idea of couple time always seemed to take a backseat.

When you think you have it all under control and that you have figured out how to effectively parent your children and still maintain your marriage, just remember that every time you turn a corner, you are going to face new challenges. These challenges will be both in the realm of parenting and in the realm of maintaining your marriage.

The Hectic Stage

This stage is a hectic time for couples and families. Multiple children usually are in the picture with multiple activities and needs. As a matter of fact, if you thought the previous stage was exhausting, you haven't seen anything yet. This period seems to be the most physically and emotionally draining of all the stages. The pressures of carpooling, school activities, jobs, church, and extracurricular activities seem never ending. Parents often become absorbed and overwhelmed with the many demands of life, and the marriage suffers.

We are faced with the reality that there really are only twenty-four hours in a day, no matter how hard we try to stretch them. Only so many of the things we have committed to do are going to fit in that already overfilled space. Something has to give. And unfortunately, it is usually our adult relationships, particularly marriage, which are the first to fall off the edge of time into the proverbial black hole.

I often compare marriage to a garden. You spend time preparing for it and cultivating it. Then it begins to grow. What you do next determines the health of the crop. You can sit back and watch it grow—and it will, weeds and all, at least for a while. But without daily attention, it will become overrun with weeds and wither from lack of water and nourishment. Or you can give the garden, and your marriage, a little attention every day, pulling the weeds while they are small and insignificant and providing the nourishment that the garden needs. If you choose this option, the harvest of your marriage will overflow. Beware: The longer you go without giving the daily attention, the more work you will have to put into your garden to get it healthy again. But once that initial work is done, a healthy garden and marriage can be easily maintained through daily attention.

It is during the early-school-years stage of parenting that the marriage garden is most likely to become neglected and overrun by weeds. You may not even realize it right away because you are so busy with everything else. One day, you have a break in the monotony and come up for a breath of fresh air. That's when you notice that the garden has become overgrown with weeds, and your spouse seems to be lost somewhere among them. Marriage suffers through this stage from a lack of nourishment and attention, and if not caught soon, it will become so overgrown with weeds that it will hardly look like the marriage garden you planted not so long ago. Give the garden of your marriage a little attention every day to keep it growing and looking beautiful.

The Survival Zone

You truly have hit the survival zone. In order to survive, you and your spouse must go into a total energy-conservation mode. Life and kids are going by at warp speed and seem to be pulling all your available energy toward them. If you are going to have any reserve energy, you will need to learn to take shortcuts wherever possible. Set your priorities and stick with them. Making your marriage relationship your top priority (second only to your relationship with God) is the key to staying connected during this stage. If you are running here and there all day long and wearing yourself out with the tasks of children, household, job, and so forth, then what do you have left at the end of the day for your spouse? A big, fat nothing! It is time to prioritize and learn to say no to one more activity. Seriously consider making some scheduling changes to lighten your daily load.

Prioritizing your schedule involves identifying which activities are most important to you and your family and saying no to everything else. This is an essential element of survival. How good are you at saying no …

☞ when the PTA calls for help at the Valentine party?

☞ when Scouts request your help on a campout?

☞ when your pastor asks you to teach a Bible study?

☞ when your child asks to have a slumber party?

☞ when your spouse asks you to have lunch?

Are you one of those people who struggles to say no and ends up feeling overcommitted and overwhelmed? What good does that do anyone? Whom do you really have trouble saying no to? Let me share with you how a friend of mine struggles with this very issue.

The Ability to Say No

David and Rhonda have been married about fourteen years and have three great kids. They have lived in the same town their whole lives and are a couple of the sweetest and friendliest people you will ever meet. As a matter of fact, soon after I met them I realized that Rhonda was one of those "so-sweet-she-could-never-say-no" kind of people. We went to church together for a few years, and I quickly noticed that Rhonda seemed to be involved in everything. She always wore a smile, but somewhere beneath that smile she often looked exhausted.

One day, I was walking in the hall at church with her when a mutual friend stopped us and asked Rhonda if she would be able to babysit for her the next day. Rhonda hesitated and then began to shake her head, saying she wasn't sure if she could. But before she could get it all out, the friend went on to explain how the kids were going to be out of school and how she just couldn't afford to take another day off work. And the next thing I heard was Rhonda saying, "Yeah, sure, I think I can make that work." And the friend was gone with a big, "Thanks. You're the greatest."

When I asked Rhonda why she agreed, she just shrugged. "I didn't have anything really important planned. And besides, she really needed me." I witnessed this pattern of events many times over the next few months.

Rhonda and I lost track of each other for awhile, but we reconnected recently, and I could see that she was still struggling with learning to say no. She was depressed, and her health was beginning to suffer. But she continued to overcommit and seemed to be on the verge of burnout. She and her husband were more distant than ever because they had so little time together between his long work hours and her myriad activities and responsibilities.

She admitted that she was headed for a meltdown, but she did not know how to stop it. She hated telling people no. She was sure that if she said no they would not like her anymore. She hated seeing the look of disappointment on people's faces and thought that by not saying no she was fixing that for them. She also did not believe that what she wanted to do was nearly as important as whatever all these other people needed. She struggled with self-esteem and did not believe that she deserved to stand up for herself, say no, and go about doing what she wanted to do. The result was that everyone around her took advantage of her and stole her away piece by piece from her husband and kids.

One day, I asked her, "So, you can't say no to anyone?"

"No, I just hate the look on their faces. Just the other day I really tried to say no and mean it. A lady at church asked me to help with VBS. I said no—well, not really. But I did make up some excuses as to why I'd better not. Do you know what she said? 'Okay, well, if you can get that worked out, will you do the five-year-old class?' And all I could do was nod my head. I'm so pathetic!"

"You're not pathetic," I assured her. "But you do need to figure this thing out before I have to come visit you in a hospital somewhere."

"What am I going to do? Why is this so hard for me?"

"Okay, let's look at this. You are telling me that you can't tell anyone no. You obviously can't say no to the people at church or to friends who need you to watch their kids. That is definitely a problem. But what about David? What did you say to him last week when he asked you if you wanted to go out on a date?"

"I told him no, of course. He knew there was no way I would have time or energy after having worked at VBS all week. I couldn't believe he was even asking."

"But I thought you said you couldn't say no to anyone?"

Rhonda sat there with her mouth open as she realized what she had just said. Obviously, she was able to tell someone no. As she thought about it, she realized that the only people she tended to say no to were her husband and kids, and they were actually the only ones she really did want to do things with. She began to understand that if you think you are not telling anyone no, you'd better reevaluate. You have to be telling *someone* no to *something* in order to continue doing everything for everyone else. That someone is most likely going to be someone right under your nose: your spouse, your kids, or yourself. When you struggle with saying no to the people around you, your most precious relationships suffer.

Rhonda's new understanding of what she was doing gave her some incentive to make some long-needed changes. She started working on saying yes to her family first and foremost. And only after checking with them would she say yes to anything or anyone else. Her husband and kids got back what was being stolen from them—their wife and mom. I know these changes have not been easy for Rhonda, and there have been some setbacks. Overall, I know she is working on it and making great progress. How do I know? Well, I called her just a couple of weeks ago to see if she could watch my kids for a day. Guess what she said? "No." I was so proud of her.

Mowing Your Own Yard

Think back to chapter 8. We talked about being responsible for what is inside your own fence and letting others be responsible for what is inside theirs. This is the stage where applying that rule is most important. Clearly define the boundaries for you and your family. Then be responsible for you and your family first and foremost. When you realize ahead of time that you are going to be pulled in a million and one directions from within your own household, you'll be less likely to commit to also being pulled in a million and two directions by someone else's household.

I'm not saying that you should not help out a friend in need or take turns carpooling or even mow your neighbors' yard once in a while. I am saying that these events should not take precedence over caring for your family. These events should be periodic and balanced. You should not be the only mom who takes all the kids to soccer practice so the other moms can run errands or rest. These events should be give-and-take so no one feels taken advantage of. Your time with your family is valuable and must be your first priority. If you are so busy helping out the whole neighborhood, what will you have left to give to your family?

Let's take this a step further. Let's say you have mastered the principle of being responsible only for what's inside your own fence, and you are not taking on excessive external responsibilities. Your family knows that they come first. Is that enough to keep your marriage strong and help you survive this hectic stage of life? Unfortunately, the answer is no.

When you seriously take a look at what is inside your fence (ignoring everyone else's yard), you will likely still feel overwhelmed. The schedules for your household can seem crammed with family members involved in everything from piano lessons to baseball and from community service to laundry. How in the world are you supposed to keep up with it all and still feel as though you are more than just a taxi service? How are you supposed to feel like a husband or wife? How are you supposed to feel like a couple when all you seem to be doing is being a parent?

Determining to keep a couple-centered marriage, not a child-centered marriage, is the key to feeling like more than just mom and dad, or worse yet, maid, chauffeur, and short-order cook. If you are going to avoid placing your marriage on the back burner for the next several years, you will have to make a conscious effort to pencil each other in to your busy schedules first. Make a commitment to say yes to your spouse as often as possible. Remember that you do not want him or her to be the most likely one to hear a "No, I don't have time for that" from you. Help your spouse to know that he or she really is your number one priority and that even the children's schedules take a backseat to what your spouse needs from you.

Learning to Take Shortcuts

Learning time-saving, energy-conserving shortcuts to anything you possibly can will be extremely helpful during this stage. Here are a few suggestions to get you thinking:

1. Use paper plates.
2. Pick out children's clothes the night before to avoid rush-hour arguments.
3. Consider having kids sleep in comfortable clothes they can wear the next day.
4. Close doors instead of cleaning rooms (especially when having company).
5. Order pizza or eat out.
6. Accept that fish sticks and green beans (or any other quick, microwave entrée) can count as a meal.
7. Hire someone to do anything you can afford to pay someone to do (clean house, do laundry,

prepare meals, mow yard). Remember, your
time is valuable and in short supply.

8. For those special occasions, buy the cake or
cupcakes instead of baking them.

9. Carpool the kids to their activities.

10. To cut back on laundry, have children wear
jeans and use bath towels more than once
before washing them.

Finding the Fun

Is this an all-doom-and-gloom phase of our lives? Absolutely
not! Some wonderful encounters occur during this stage. These
early-school-age years can be an enjoyable time between parents
and children. The kids have become more independent and do not
require parental attention 24/7. This allows for parents to make
some private time more easily than in the earlier stage. The possibility of sleeping in late (or at least later) on Saturday morning,
closing (and locking) the bedroom door for some private "mom-
and-dad" time, and taking a walk—just the two of you—can again
become a reality.

This is also a time when the children really enjoy being with
their parents and siblings. They look forward to family outings,
game night, meals together, and family discussions. Of all the
stages, this is the most family interactive. As kids and parents spend
time together, the feelings of closeness and bonding grow. This
drawing closer of the family unit has the effect of drawing the couple closer together as well.

As I write this, my family is smack-dab in the middle of this
stage—and I love it! Yes, the challenges are there and the schedules
are in constant need of pruning. But our time together as a family
is the most fun it has ever been. One of our favorite activities is family game night. We schedule at least one night a week for this, but
it usually ends up being as many nights as we can possibly work it

in. Even our youngest, Talon (who is five), really enjoys this time together. As a matter of fact, he is often the initiator of game time. The laughter that fills our house during an intense game of "Spoons," where we fight over that very last spoon, is one of the most precious things ever.

I love that my children cannot seem to get enough of family time and constantly want us to be together doing something. I know this time will pass all too soon, and I want to savor as much of it as I possibly can. It is also true that strong positive family time together can actually make you and your spouse feel closer. I know that when Jim and I have had a great evening enjoying each other and the kids, we seem to be naturally drawn to each other even more after the kids go to bed.

Ten Tips for Staying Connected through the Hectic Times

1. Commit to remaining a couple-centered marriage. Keeping your marriage as the number one priority is at the top of this list for a reason: It is the most important thing you can do for each other. The busier you get, the more precious this time together will become. Make this the most important appointment in your planner, and do not let anything short of a natural disaster change it.

2. Allow family time to draw you closer. A sense of family is the greatest in this stage and can serve as an additional connection point for you and your spouse. As the family laughs and plays together, the family unit is strengthened. The marital bond can be enhanced through any and all positive encounters, including those that involve you and your children loving each other. So why not capitalize on the strong desire to spend time together? Let your children be a part of keeping the two of you connected.

3. Prune your schedule. Take time to evaluate how much you have going on as individuals and as a family. Be willing to cut back on the activities your children are involved in as well as your own extracurricular activities. Although our society may not agree, it really is not necessary to fill every spare minute. Taking time to relax and be together is valuable in itself. It may be helpful to sit down together each week and look over the next week's activities. You can use that time to evaluate your priorities and make sure everyone is on the same page. But more importantly, you can determine together when your life is getting "too full."

4. Learn to say yes to each other. Avoid the trap of your spouse and kids being the ones most likely to hear no from you. Whenever you possibly can, say yes to your spouse's invitations to spend time together, doing whatever you can think of to do. Learning to say no to outside events and activities will allow you even more time together.

5. Take advantage of your children's growing independence. As they grow, they actually like to show you that they can be responsible for themselves, and sometimes their younger siblings, at least for short periods of time. Use this to carve out additional couple time by taking a walk, locking the bedroom door for some "mommy-and-daddy" time, and sleeping in on Saturday mornings.

6. Hire a young neighbor to play with your kids. Consider finding a young (twelve- or thirteen-year-old) yet responsible child in your neighborhood to watch your kids for a short time, even if you are not going to leave the house. You will still be close by and available in case of emergencies, but you won't have to be watching your kids the whole time. You can send them to the backyard or to a nearby park for an hour or so while the two of you have some adult-only time.

7. Keep talking. Never underestimate the power of conversation. It will draw you closer and keep you connected if done correctly. Remember to talk about something other than your kids. They already infiltrate every aspect of your life—why not take some time to get to know each other all over again by asking each other questions. Or maybe just take time to discuss your thoughts and feelings about what is going on in the world, what God has been teaching you recently, or where you would like to be five or ten years down the road.

8. Take time for yourself. When the world around you seems to be draining you, one way to revitalize yourself is to do something just for you. Remember, you cannot give what you do not possess. So if you are running on empty and have no energy left, you will not be able to give to your spouse or your children. Take time to do whatever it is that helps you refuel yourself. You may want to play a game of golf, take a bubble bath, go for a walk, or read a magazine.

9. Put the kids to bed (or at least in their bedrooms) early. Children need more sleep than we realize and can also benefit from learning to spend some quiet time alone. So, when you and your sweetheart need some extra time together, send the kids to their rooms. They can either go to sleep, read a book, or listen to music while you and your spouse enjoy some special time just for the two of you.

10. Give your marriage and your spouse daily attention. If you do not want your marriage garden to become overgrown with weeds, be sure to pay attention to your spouse every day. Doing something special, saying thank you, sending a love note, or calling in the middle of the day can be that little extra attention that your spouse needs to feel treasured by you.

Coming Up Next ...

Third quarter is about to begin. You have made it more than halfway and are starting the downhill slide. But do not expect it to be easy. Although many of the physically draining responsibilities begin to lighten up during this stage, they are replaced with emotionally draining events. Some of the biggest challenges of the third quarter revolve around conflicts between teens and parents, and then often between the parents themselves. Chapter 13 will help you identify the three biggest areas of conflict and provide suggestions to help resolve these.

CHAPTER THIRTEEN

HELP! GET ME OUT OF HERE!

Third Quarter: The Teen Years

Chuck: Chuck Itall here again with the latest on the "Game of the Century." Well, Genie, what a game it has been so far! Both teams made a good showing throughout the first half and seem ready to get on with the game. With halftime finished, both teams are back on the field, and we're ready to start the third quarter. The Kids team seems to have gathered fresh energy going into this quarter and is already taunting the Parents team from the sidelines. Any idea what that's all about?

Genie: Yes, Chuck, from what I can tell, these kids are ready to pull out all the stops and start calling the shots. I caught up with some of them during halftime, and they informed me that the third quarter was going to be theirs. They say they spent the first half of this game really studying their opponents, and they've

CHILDPROOFING YOUR MARRIAGE

been able to determine their weak spots. They are ready to capitalize on that knowledge and plan a subtle attack that will really hit 'em where it hurts.

Chuck: From what I can see, that is exactly what they're doing. The Kids team has just swept down the field with very little opposition from the Parents. As a matter of fact, the members of the Parents team seemed dumbfounded at the skill and precision of this attack and are currently arguing among themselves.

Genie: As we listen in on the on-field microphone, we can hear the Parents actively blaming each other for allowing that play to get through. Oh my, this is looking nasty. If this Parents team doesn't pull it together quick, the Kids are going to score big. Hold on, the Parents just called for a time-out, and we are only a couple of minutes into the quarter. Maybe it is for the best, if they can get this thing worked out before continuing. Well, folks, we'll be right back after these messages.

The "Runaway" Impulse

If you ever want to run away and escape from parenting, it will be now, in the middle of the most challenging of all the parenting stages. As our children grow and mature (and they do mature eventually), they develop their own sense of self and start to pull away from the family unit. With hormones raging, peer pressure growing, and self-esteem faltering, teens will challenge parents and the marital bond in a brand-new way. Conflicts between teens and parents quickly turn into conflicts between the parents. Couples who have not already discussed and reached a point of agreement on the basic conflict areas between teens and their parents will be in danger at this stage.

Even couples who have done well in maneuvering the earlier stages of parenting may find themselves faltering during the teen years. Parents are likely to be more at odds with each other, especially in regard to setting and enforcing family rules. Schedules continue to be busy during the first part of this stage, but the crunch will ease once the kids start to drive. However, the stress of constantly being a taxi driver is replaced with the stress of worrying about teen drivers out on their own.

Couples may take each other for granted more during this stage than earlier stages. They may say to themselves, "We've made it this far; now we are home free." That, in addition to the possible added stress of having aging parents of their own, financial concerns about college, premenopausal symptoms, and personal retirement plans, can make the third quarter of marriage more difficult than any other. As a result of all these stresses, couples must commit themselves to supporting each other and making time for each other here just as much—maybe more so—than in earlier stages.

Throughout this chapter, we will discuss some of the unique challenges that come along with parenting teenagers. First we will talk about the three main areas of conflict between the teen and the parents. And then we will spend some time discussing what to do when your teen *really* rebels. And finally, I will present you with "Ten Tips for Surviving the Teen Years." Let me set the stage for this first section by sharing a story with you about one particular family's struggle with raising their two teenage sons. I think you will soon see how the Franklin family could just as easily be any one of our families while we are raising teenagers.

The Franklins

Ben and Barb Franklin had been married for nineteen years when I first met them. As they sat in my office they informed me that overall they felt they were doing fine as a couple—that was not why they were here. They were here to discuss their two sons, ages seventeen and fifteen, and seek treatment for them. When I asked what the problem seemed to be, Barb talked practically nonstop for the next forty-five minutes about all the problems they were having with their boys. Ben interjected periodically, and then only briefly ,before Barb was off and running again.

She felt overwhelmed and seemed to need some validation that there really was a problem. When Ben attempted to interrupt, he was often saying something like, "Yeah, Sam did do that, but you know, he's really a good kid," or, "Jake is having trouble doing his chores, but he is studying hard and trying to keep his grades up." It was obvious that these two parents had significant differences of opinion in regard to their boys. I agreed to meet with the boys for a couple of sessions and then asked the parents to come back to discuss what the best treatment would be. They agreed.

Over the next couple of weeks, I met with each of the boys and got their take on what was going on. And do you know what? They each had a completely different opinion, although theirs matched each other's much more closely than their parents' did. Both Jake and Sam expressed a high degree of tension and conflict within the household, and although they did accept some of this as being between the two of them, they both felt the majority of the fighting was coming from their parents.

In separate sessions, each of the boys made significant and similar observations. One of these was, "Mom thinks she has to control everything and everyone." She was constantly telling them what to do, when to do it, and how it needed to be done. She monitored their every move and checked up on them so much that it had become a joke with their friends. She was still asking about their schoolwork every day, even though they had proved to be good students and self-motivated. They felt she did not trust them to make any of their own decisions. Jake even stated, "I'm going to be going away to college next year. Is she going to go with me? I would really like to spend this year learning to do more things myself."

Another common statement the boys made was, "Dad is a pushover." Although Barb seemed to be into everything, Ben was just the opposite. When they asked him if they could go to a friend's house, he would smile and say, "Of course. Have fun." He never asked any details about whose house, what for, or when they would be back. They loved this. As a matter of fact, since they knew how Barb would have handled the same request, they found themselves waiting until Barb was gone to ask Ben for what they wanted. On more than one occasion, they returned from the friend's house to find Barb and Ben in a knock-down-drag-out fight about why Ben had not asked more questions. Actually, it was not a knock-down kind of fight because Ben would not fight. He would just sit there quietly while Barb ranted and raved, and then he would apologize and say he would try to do better next time—but he never did.

One final common point brought out by both boys was, "Neither one of them ever follows through with what they say." This was mainly in reference to discipline and consequences as a result of their disobedience. Because the parents obviously did not agree on the appropriate punishments, they didn't support each other in this area. One of them (usually Barb) would set a punishment (most often it was being grounded from going out with friends or being banned from the computer) for something one of the boys had done wrong, in her opinion. When she told Ben, he would say something like, "Don't you think that's a little strong?" or, "What was so wrong with that?" and the boys knew they would be off the hook.

Barb sometimes would set a punishment herself and later seem to forget it. She would walk by and see one of them on the computer when he shouldn't have been and not say a word. So the boys had pretty much decided that the worst punishment they would get for just about any offense was having to endure their mom yelling at them—then in reality it was over.

After these few sessions, I was ready to get these parents back into my office for a pow-wow. When Ben and Barb returned, they were expecting me to tell them how screwed up their boys were and just exactly how we were going to fix them. But that is not what I had to say.

What I shared with these parents was that they had raised a couple of fairly normal teenage boys. Barb started to object, but I quickly asked her to hear me out. I explained that I agreed with her that many of the behaviors the boys were exhibiting were inappropriate and should not be accepted.

"But I thought you said they were normal," Barb interjected.

"I did, and they are," I continued.

I went on to explain that it is normal for teenagers to disobey, push the limits, flat-out rebel, and attempt to get by with whatever they possibly can. The problem often does not lie in the teens' behavior; it lies in the parents' response to that behavior.

I spent the rest of the session sharing with Ben and Barb what their sons had said about them and their parenting skills. I helped them understand that as long as the two of them were not acting as a team, their boys would continue to push the limits, and eventually this could be a full-fledged and possibly dangerous rebellion.

Once this was out on the table, I began to ask more questions about their relationship. Although they had said that they were doing "fine" as a couple in the first session, it soon became evident that this was not accurate. When they got right down to it, there had been significant tension between them ever since the boys were little. They often fought about how to discipline them or what constituted "normal" boy behavior. Ben felt that Barb just had no concept that boys are different from girls. She had not had any brothers and really no exposure to boys as she was growing up. So when Ben would roughhouse and wrestle with the boys when they were little, she would get upset and tell him to stop.

They also argued about what the boys should be allowed to do, such as what kinds of movies they could see, when they could spend the night at a friend's house, or how far from the house they could ride their bikes. It seemed as though everything was a battle, and because Ben hated conflict, he eventually just stopped arguing. Resentments began to build up, and Ben admitted that, because he still did not agree with Barb, he would often end up sabotaging Barb's punishment.

Barb also admitted to underlying feelings of resentment toward Ben for his passive nature with the boys. She felt like a single parent when it came to discipline. He seemed to be around only for the fun times with the boys and would leave the rest to her. There were times when she had just wanted to give up because Ben would not support her and always seemed to take the boys' side.

By the end of the session, both Ben and Barb realized that they were the problem more than the boys. Not only were they not parenting their sons, they were destroying their marriage. They were actually able to thank each other for being honest, and they agreed to work on changing their relationship so they could become a team in parenting their children.

Three Main Areas of Conflict

Although there are infinite possibilities for areas where a teen and parents can and will disagree, there are actually only three main categories that everything else falls into. The major areas of conflict between the teen and parents relate to

1. the amount of freedom to be allowed,
2. the appropriate amount of responsibility, and
3. the definition of effective discipline.

We would expect that teens would have their own views of what is appropriate in each of these areas. Furthermore, we would expect that those views would not match parental views. However, when the parental views do not agree with each other, that is where the real problem lies. Teens are masterful at finding the parenting team's weak spot and going right for it. If you do not agree in a certain area, they know it (probably better than you do) and will use it to their advantage. As parents of teens, you must learn to discuss your differences in each of these three main areas and work to reach compromises that both of you can be comfortable with. This could take some time and energy. Be willing to continue the negotiating and brainstorming until you can reach a mutually satisfying resolution. Avoid the trap of giving in just to get it over with or because it seems too hard. If you give in, knowing that you really do not agree with the decision, you may later find yourself undermining the other parent's authority, causing additional marital conflicts. The couple should agree not to make any decisions in any of these three main areas without complete parental agreement. Keep working through options until the two of you can find one that you both feel comfortable with. I would recommend that you use the ECHO communications skills discussed in chapter 6 to help you with this process.

The earlier you work out these three major areas of conflict, the easier it will be for both you and your teens. Once the children realize that you two are in agreement and that they can't "divide and conquer," they will begin to push the limits less often (but they will still push).

Speaking of pushing, we said earlier that it is a teen's expected behavior to push the limits. But what happens when a teen pushes too far, when the "normal" pushing turns into a complete and open rebellion against everything the teen has been taught? How does rebellion affect the marital team?

Assigning Fault

About two years ago, I sat face to face with the most rebellious and angry teenager I had ever met. Ami was sixteen years old and spitting bullets and throwing fiery glances at me the whole time her mother, Sarah, was explaining, "We just don't know what else to do. She won't listen to anything we tell her."

"Why should I listen to a stupid woman like you? You don't know anything about me or my life, so just butt out and let me do what I want to do. You can't stop me anyway, so just get off my back!"

And that was just the first couple of minutes of the session. Wow! I had no idea what I was in for. As the session progressed, the language and name-calling got worse. Eventually, I asked the mother to step into the waiting room. I hoped that once she was gone, Ami would calm down and want to talk. I was wrong. She just turned her anger onto me.

I allowed her to vent (not that I could have stopped her if I'd wanted to) for several more minutes. In the process of this tirade, I found out that she

☞ had a boyfriend that her parents did not
     approve of;
☞ was having sex with him "just because it makes
     them mad";
☞ drank and smoked a little weed and was hop-
     ing to try some of the hard stuff as soon as she
     could get her hands on it;
☞ hated God, Jesus, church, and anything else
     her parents had been cramming down her
     throat all her life.

That is a pretty good start on a complete and open rebellion, don't you think?

By the end of the session, I knew that I would likely never see this teen again because anything her parents wanted her to do was exactly what she was not going to do. My only hope was to make it her choice. I told both Ami and her mother that it was up to Ami if she ever came back and that actually I expected her not to. I encouraged Sarah to come back on her own for support and suggestions about how to best deal with this situation, and she agreed. We made an appointment for Sarah but not for Ami. I wished her well and said good-bye.

The next week Sarah came in with her husband, John, and we

spent the time discussing how each of them felt about what Ami was doing. Although I never asked either of them why they thought Ami was acting this way, they felt compelled to tell me. I soon learned that they were each convinced that the other one was to blame for this rebellious acting out. John felt Sarah was to blame because she was always dragging Ami and her siblings to church "every time the doors were open" and because she was always spending money and buying Ami new things that she didn't even need.

Sarah, on the other hand, retaliated that John was actually the one to blame for Ami's rebellion and promiscuity because he was never around. He was always working late and gone on business trips. He never gave Ami the male attention that she needed, and now she was getting it from some boy they had never even met. And they had not met the boyfriend because John's anger was always so unpredictable that the kids never wanted to invite their friends over.

After listening to this exchange, I realized where Ami had learned to be vicious with her tongue. I stopped them and validated that it is a scary time in anyone's life when your child is rebelling against everything you have ever taught her. I helped them share what they had each hoped for and dreamed of regarding Ami, and as they did, they began to soften. I reminded them that no parent is perfect and that each of us could look back on something we wish we had done better or differently. But at this stage of the game, blaming each other for their child's choices would do nothing but tear the two of them apart. They agreed and apologized to each other.

Both John and Sarah admitted that most of what they had said was either not true or was exaggerated. John admitted that church was just as important to him as it was to Sarah. But in the previous four years, his job had taken him out of town often and he worked long hours, so he had not been able to attend with his family very often. Two years earlier, when Ami started fighting about going to church, Sarah was on her own to deal with it. And he was actually glad that she had chosen to make Ami continue to attend.

Sarah admitted that even though John's job required a lot of overnight traveling, he had done his best to work that around the children's special events. She said he was a good dad and really tried to make himself available whenever possible. She started crying and said, "I guess I just wanted someone to blame. I just can't figure out what went wrong!"

We spent the rest of that session and several more helping this couple regain their sense of closeness and realize there was only so much they could do to redirect Ami's behaviors. The most important thing was to parent consistently and, in this case, with some "tough love" strategies. Other than that, they needed to work on their marriage and on helping each other grow together, not further apart, through this crisis. Instead of blaming each other or themselves for what might have happened in the past, they committed to focus on what they could do right now and in the future.

As much as I would like to tell you there's a happy ending to this story, I can't—at least not with regard to Ami. I did see her a couple more times. Once she realized that no one was going to make her return to see me, she made an appointment and came in. Even that seemed to be some sort of a rebellion to her, because I had said I expected her not to come back. So coming back was the opposite, and therefore rebellious, in her mind. She had just turned seventeen and felt as though that was her ticket to freedom. She moved out of her parents' house and in with her boyfriend and his mom. She was starting a job and thinking about quitting school and getting a GED so she could get on with her life and have some fun.

I knew no amount of talking and rationalizing was going to make any difference to this girl. She would have to learn her lessons through the University of Hard Knocks. But that did not stop me from trying. The last I heard, Ami was still trying to make her own way the hard way and had very little contact with her parents. But they keep the door open to her (with some well-defined boundaries), pray for her, and go about focusing on their relationship and the two children still in the home. My heart went out to Ami, and still does. But, like her parents, all I can do now is pray for her.

The Blame Game

The teenage years are a time of emotional turmoil for parents. They may be faced with feelings of failure and inadequacy when their teens exert their independence and start to rebel against the parents' set of values. Although this is an expected part of raising teenagers, it can become particularly difficult when the rebellion is extreme. If they are not careful, parents can begin to blame each other for poor choices the teen is making. This "blame game" is destructive to the marital bond.

We must understand and accept that we are all imperfect human beings and therefore imperfect parents. We all have made numerous mistakes by the time our kids reach their teens. So if we are all making mistakes, why aren't all teenagers experiencing extreme rebellion? Why are some adolescents more compliant, responsible, and mature than others? The extent of their rebellion has more to do with their unique personalities and ways of coping with the world than what their parents did or did not do.

Of course, there are some situations in which one or both parents may have done or not done something that contributed to a child's rebellion. The best you can do at that point is to admit your mistake and seek forgiveness. In 1 John 1:9, God promised to forgive those who confess their sins: "If we confess our sins, he is faithful and just and will forgive us our sins and purify us from all unrighteousness." You do not have to continue to beat yourself up for a past mistake. Forgive yourself and move forward to figure out what can be done now to change the situation.

When you think about it, what purpose does it serve to blame yourself or your spouse—or anyone else for that matter—for something that happened in the past? It will not change anything, and the one thing you need most when your child is rebelling is change. So forgive each other if forgiveness is warranted; otherwise spend your energy working on a possible solution to the situations, and spend time praying for your wayward child.

Ten Tips for Thriving through the Teen Years

1. Set and agree on family rules. The biggest conflicts between parents have to do with three basic family rules. The two of you need to set these boundaries and rules together and be in complete agreement about how they will be stated and enforced. This is part of the teamwork of parenting and will greatly cut down on the conflicts between the two of you, as well as on areas where your teen can drive a wedge between you.

2. Start the letting-go process now. I've heard it said, "You gave them roots, now give them wings." What a great saying! You have spent more than a decade instilling in your children the basic values and principles you wanted them to learn; now it is time to see how much they retained. Giving them a chance to prove themselves as well as possibly making their own mistakes is all part of helping them grow up. You can still be there to support them, but starting to let them go now will make the next stage go more smoothly for all of you.

3. Enjoy your teen. Many couples have shared that although the teen years have their challenges, that time is definitely not all bad. They have shared about how much they have enjoyed having these energetic, playful, and talented kids around their home. They seem to bring a feeling of excitement to everything, and the whole family, including the marriage, seems to be energized by them.

4. Coparent in all things. You must parent together! Your teens know you well and are masterful at driving wedges between parents who do not parent cooperatively. Coparenting involves more than just disciplining together, although that is one of the most important parts. It also involves the two of you agreeing to keep each other informed about schedules, decisions, and general progress. Agree between the two of you that you will not keep secrets from each other regarding your children. Be sure to inform the kids of that agreement as well.

5. Keep the lines of communication open. This refers to the communication between you and your spouse as well as between the two of you and your teen. Check in daily with each other about how the day has gone and also about plans for the next few days. Talk about how school is going, what your teen's favorite song is, and why he or she wants dyed hair. The more you talk, the closer you will all be, and the fewer the conflicts you will experience.

6. Choose your battles carefully! This applies to both the marital relationship as well as the parent–child relationship. Work on developing tolerance, flexibility, and patience. Try to allow whatever you can because there will be plenty that you cannot allow. When you must battle, remember to fight FAIR (see chapter 7). Another rule of thumb is to work on saying yes as often as you possibly can to things like tasteful piercing, changing hairstyle and color, music, activities, friends, and so forth. The more you say yes, the more your "no" will stand out when you have to use it. Teens will also be more likely to respect a "no" when they do not feel as though they hear that every time they turn around. Many parents seem to have developed a habit of saying no before thinking about it and then later may change their minds. Take the time to consider what is being asked, and say yes whenever you possibly can.

7. Keep dating. Hopefully by this stage, you have dating down to an art. Your once-a-week date night is one of the most important times you can spend together. Schedule this into your calendar and hold it sacred. By the end of this stage, your teens may be dating, too—you definitely do not want them to be having all the fun.

8. Start a hobby or other activity together. Start using the extra time that you are going to have as the kids become more independent to put some extra time into your marriage. Find a hobby or activity that the two of you have always wanted to do but never had the time for; start doing it together. This will help you continue to be couple focused and begin the process of redefining your relationship before the empty nest hits.

9. Put out the "Do Not Disturb" sign. One of teenagers' favorite statements is, "I just want some privacy." They often want to be left alone in their bedrooms to do whatever it is that teenagers do. So why not put that same philosophy to use for you? Schedule regular "Do Not Disturb" times when you and your spouse can be alone and uninterrupted in your room—and do whatever it is that married couples do.

10. Develop an outside support network. Spend time with other adults who are also parenting teens or have already been through this stage. This can be a great source of encouragement, advice, and validation. Use these times together to share openly about both the ups and the downs of raising teens. Give each other permission to talk about the rough times instead of keeping these to yourselves. It will help to know that you are not alone when it comes to the challenges of teenagers.

Coming Up Next ...

As much as our children have created great stress, conflict, and worry over the past several years, most of us hate to see them go. We love them and have been focusing on providing the best for them for almost two decades. Of course it is going to be an adjustment when they leave home. The fourth quarter of parenting begins as your first child leaves the nest and you are faced with not only letting him or her go but also with adjusting to having more time with your spouse. Even if this is something you have been anxiously awaiting, you will have adjustments to make. And as you do so, you will realize your relationship is coming full circle. You are about to experience "just the two of us" all over again. Enjoy!

CHAPTER FOURTEEN

YOU DON'T LOOK LIKE THE PERSON I MARRIED!

Fourth Quarter: From First Child Leaving to Empty Nest

Chuck: Well, Genie, here we are entering the fourth quarter of the "Game of the Century," and we see the game beginning to wind down. Both teams seem to be doing well and are holding their own better than in earlier quarters. As the clock ticks down, we can't help but wonder what these teams will be like after the final whistle blows.

Genie: Chuck, I think the two teams on the field are wondering the same thing. The Kids team was overheard during the last break saying they just can't wait for this game to be over. They are ready to move on and do new things, but they realize they still need the Parents team around if they hope to finish the game. On the other hand, the Parents team seems to have some mixed feelings about entering this final stage of the game. Sometimes they have been heard saying they, too, are ready for the game to be over and are looking forward to life after the game. At other times, they have been heard yelling at the referee to put more time back on the game clock, stating that it is going too fast and that they aren't ready for the game to be over.

Chuck: This turmoil for the Parents team seems to be contagious. In a game just a few weeks ago, one member of the Parents team was seen clinging to a member of the Kids team after the final whistle had blown. The Parents player was doing everything possible to drag the Kids player back onto the field. This was both a humorous and pathetic sight. I guess that Parents player didn't realize he would be seeing the whole Kids team after the game for a postgame social gathering. Maybe if someone had told him, this embarrassing encounter would never have occurred.

Genie: Let's just hope we don't see that kind of reaction at the end of the game today.

The Difficulty of the Empty Nest

In the past two decades, statistics have indicated that divorce rates are on the rise for couples who have been married thirty or more years.[1] Does this surprise you? Many of us would think that by the time a couple had made it thirty years or more they should have it all figured out and be "home free." It would seem to those of us still in the middle years of parenting that the stage where the kids are finally out from under foot would be nothing short of heavenly. For some parents, it seems that things could only get better once the stress of the children is gone. But for others, the idea of their children, whom they have loved and enjoyed for so long, no longer being in the house is nothing short of devastating. Right now, I do not even want to think about these precious little ones not being in the home to greet me with a great big "Mommy's home!" Maybe that's why God put the teenage years right before this stage, to help parents become better ready to send them out on their own. Regardless of whether you are ready to release your children into the world or you are reluctantly doing so, you cannot avoid experiencing the hole that children leave behind. Many a couple has spent their entire married life raising children and making those children the center of their world. As they did so, they likely neglected their marriage, and eventually it began to wither and die. Perhaps at some point the only connection the couple had was the children. All of their communication centered on the kids in one way or another. Maybe they discussed Kathy's progress in school, how to deal with Tom's breaking curfew, how they were going to afford college, or countless other topics related to the children.

Some empty-nest couples soon find that their focus on the children was an effective way for them to avoid areas of conflict within the marriage. What do you think happens when the children, who have been serving as buffers or distracters for the parents' problems, finally leave the home? That's right, the conflicts between the parents increase. Old unresolved issues begin to rear their ugly heads again and tension mounts. If the couple has not developed healthy conflict-resolution skills, this could become the kiss of death to the marriage.

Another area that becomes evident once the children leave the home is the issue of self-identity. Often, one or both parents have invested their entire selves into the role of parent. Once that role is over, you have nothing left. It is like placing all your eggs in one basket or planting only one crop in your garden. If the basket turns over or the crop is attacked by parent-eating bugs, what do you have left to sustain you? Nothing. Entering the empty-nest stage of marriage feeling like a great big nothing can cause an additional sense of depression and worthlessness.

Adjusting to the Empty Nest

This chapter focuses on helping you learn to let go of the children and reconnect as a couple. Even if you are picking up this book as you enter this stage of parenting, don't worry, there is still hope. You have made it this far; that says something. Regardless of how much or how little you worked to stay connected through the parenting years, you will have new adjustments once the children are gone.

This stage is unique in many ways. The main adjustments of the other stages centered on having less time together and juggling additional pressures. This stage requires you to adjust to having more time together with fewer distractions. Although this may sound like a good problem to have, it can be the end of a marriage that has drifted apart. I want to share with you three things you need to address in order to move through this stage successfully. The first is the need for you to accept and validate each other's feelings of loss and grief. The second has to do with redefining your relationship. And finally, we will address learning how to build a new relationship with your now adult children. Let's take each one of these separately.

Feelings of Loss and Grief

Regardless of how difficult the parenting years have been and how relieved you may expect to feel once the children have left the nest, you will also experience some feelings of loss and grief. How could you not? You have spent at least the past eighteen years of your life (and for most of us, it will be longer than that) loving, cuddling, chasing, teaching, arguing, and worrying, and then loving some more. These creatures we call children have brought us immeasurable joy mixed with stress beyond belief. We feel blessed to have had them for the years that we did. But now it is time to let them go. Of course we will experience feelings of grief and a sense of loss.

A wide range of emotions is normal as you watch your children grow up, move out, and start lives of their own. As a couple, you likely will have different experiences and feelings around this phase of your life. Taking time to share these feelings with each other will help you grow closer. Focus on understanding and validating how your spouse feels, even if that is not how you feel. Accept these differences and be there to support each other.

Be patient with each other through this adjustment. It is not going to happen overnight. As a matter of fact, it may take many months. If Sammy leaves for college in August, don't expect everything to be back to normal by October; that will not be the case. Be patient; you will begin to adjust to and accept this new phase of life.

During this stage, you also may experience additional feelings of loss, grief, and insecurity separate from those related to the children leaving home. This is a stage of your life where the outside forces in your life, such as mid-life issues, a realization that career dreams may not have been met, retirement, aging or dying parents, menopause, and personal aging and health issues, are all hitting hard and fast. It is important to share with each other the extent of your emotional reactions to all the events in your life in order to avoid additional feelings of isolation.

Encourage each other to talk about the changes the two of you are experiencing, and focus on validating these feelings in your spouse. Be careful not to minimize your husband's or wife's feelings. If he shares that he's scared to retire because he's not sure the two of you are financially secure or if she opens up and tells you she's worried that the kids will never come home to visit, avoid the temptation to "fix" feelings. Don't tell him, "Of course we're prepared; we've been saving for years." Don't respond to her with, "You know that's not true; they'll probably be back more than we want them to." Even if these are accurate statements, when your spouse is sharing a feeling of hurt or fear, your most loving response would be one of validating by listening and indicating that you understand that he or she could be feeling that way. There may be time for fixing and encouraging in the near future, but if you jump there too quickly, your spouse will feel invalidated.

Redefining Your Relationship

The need to redefine your relationship is something that all couples go through as they hit this stage. However, this will be most difficult for those couples who have spent the past decade or two being completely child-focused. Once the children are gone, you may find yourself living with a stranger because you did not take time to stay connected. Even couples who did focus on growing their marriage while they were parenting will have some redefining to do.

As you define what marriage looks like now that the kids are gone, you will begin to set new goals and share new hopes and expectations. You no doubt have been setting and resetting goals throughout your marriage, and this is no different; it is time, once again, to reevaluate your goals and consider new ones. Think about both your individual goals for this second half of your marriage as well as some new couple goals. Individually you may find that one of you is ready to retire and slow down, while the other is considering taking a part-time job or getting some new training. Remember, different is not wrong. Talk about these possible differences and how they can be accommodated into your couple goals. As you set new goals for yourself and your relationship, what you need from your spouse may change. Be sure to share these changing needs openly. As you discuss your new goals and dreams, you may realize that you need to make changes in your previous role definitions and in the division of labor around your house.

I remember watching Jim's parents' relationship and roles

change after we married. Jim is the baby of his family and was the last to leave the nest. Not long after we married, Jim's dad, George, retired from his job. He had worked nights and slept days for as long as Jim could remember. His time and therefore his duties around the home were minimal. Jim's mother, Barbara, had spent her life focusing on raising the children and taking care of the home. All of that was about to change.

With no children at home to care for, Barbara was seriously considering getting a part-time job. Then George retired and started being home all the time—and that clinched it; she went to work. They used to joke that Barbara had to go to work to avoid killing George. But in reality, she was simply not used to his being home all the time, and she wanted to do something more with her time.

Their roles seemed to change radically overnight. I remember going home for a visit shortly after all these changes occurred and being surprised to walk into their kitchen and see George standing at the sink doing dishes. This was such a foreign sight to me that I had to run out to the car and get my camera. I was sure I would need a picture to prove that I really saw what I thought I saw. I still have that picture, but I do not need it anymore. This was not a one-time event. It was a change in roles and responsibilities that occurred in their home that helped them each better adjust to the ever-changing seasons of marriage.

As you work to redefine your relationship and possibly change your roles, remember to keep the lines of communication open. Talk about your hopes, dreams, desires, and fears. Work to reach a compromise if there is a difference in what each of you wants to accomplish. Strike a balance between self, couple, and social time that works for both of you. But most of all, learn to enjoy the time you now have together.

Interacting with Your Adult Children

One final area of adjustment is relating to your children now that they are adults. For those of you who have been dreaming of the day when you and your child would be able to be just friends, now is the day. Once you are no longer responsible for parenting your children (and this may not be until after college for some of you), then you have the freedom to develop a friendship. I'm sure you have already been laying the foundation of this kind of a relationship over the past several years by working to keep the lines of communication open between you and your child. You also may already have several points of interest in common on which to continue to grow your friendship. The main difference in your relationship now will be that you are no longer responsible for the choices your children make or the consequences that result. You will move away from being a parent but still make yourself available to be an advisor when your children seek your advice. But remember, just because your children ask for your thoughts, opinions, or advice, this does not mean that they will follow that advice. They are learning to make their own decisions; let them.

Another aspect has to do with how you handle the expansion of your family circle. As your children develop their own lives, they may marry and have children of their own. You now will not only be forming a new adult–adult relationship with your child, but you will be learning how to share him or her with a new "most important" person. Deciding in advance how you want to open your family up to its new members to make them feel welcome will help strengthen your relationship with your child.

Ten Steps to Reclaiming Your Empty-nest Marriage

1. Fill the hole. Take time even before the last child actually moves out to discuss how the two of you would like to fill the space your kids leave behind. This should include the physical space within your home that will no longer be needed to house your kids. Talk about what you would like to do with that extra room, and make plans to do it. Also include in your discussion how you would each like to fill the time space. Your kids likely have been taking up large portions of the time available to you. Talk about how you would like to fill that time. Do you have a dream or goal that you've always wanted to accomplish? Talk about it, and consider doing it. Focus on finding activities that you both enjoy and can do together. The possibilities are endless, so have fun dreaming and then make that dream a reality.

2. Enjoy the chance to be spontaneous again. There are no babysitters to hire, baseball practices to get back for, or kids to check in with. You have finally reached the stage where you get to do what you want to do, when you want to do it, and how you want to do it. Your life is yours again. So go and have some fun at the drop of a hat. If you can think about it, you can do it. Seriously consider just saying yes on a whim, and just go for it.

3. Let go of the past. Remember the rearview mirror? It is just there for perspective, not to keep you stuck. Share your memories with each other, but don't get stuck in the belief that all the good times are in the past. You have a bright new future ahead—focus on that. As you work to put the past behind you, you may find that you have unresolved issues to deal with. Do this in a safe and forgiving environment. As you talk about some of your past hurts, remember to apply the principles of FAIR fighting (see chapter 7), because you are more likely to be willing to engage in these conversations if you are assured that they will not get out of hand. As you resolve and forgive these past hurts, you will begin to move into your future together refreshed and renewed.

4. Renew your romance and enjoy newfound sexual freedom. It has finally arrived, the day so many of you have been waiting for, the day that sexual freedom returns to your home. There are no babies crying, no little kids running around, no teenagers down the hall, no distractions, interruptions, or excuses. Just plain old freedom to enjoy each other to the full. As you take time to renew your romance and sexual relationship, be sure to talk about changes in your needs and desires that may have occurred over the years. Be willing to talk openly about what you like and do not like, but most of all, be willing to get creative and experiment to find the most satisfying physical relationship you have ever had.

5. Don't be afraid to communicate. With more time on your hands, you may find yourselves with time to talk but nothing to talk about. One or both of you may be afraid to talk because of a belief that talking will lead to arguing. Commit to each other to keep conversations light and comfortable at first. As your skills develop, you can go on to deeper topics. Work on developing a list of things to talk about that will help you avoid the "What do you want to talk about?" "I don't know. What do you want to talk about?" cycle. This cycle often frustrates couples and keeps them from talking. Here are some topics to get you started:

If money were no option, where would you like to travel?

What do you think heaven will be like?

What is your happiest memory?

How do you experience feeling loved by me?

What's one thing you have always wanted to do but never have?

(My book *Discovering the Treasure of Marriage*[2] has a list of one hundred conversation starters to help you continue with this.)

6. Focus on the positives. Attitude is everything (especially in this stage) and what you choose to focus on determines your attitude. As you enter this stage, resolve to keep focused on the positives, both about your spouse and your new phase of life. If you are going to spend time thinking about the past, do so by focusing on the positive memories. But don't stay there; move into the present and consider the future as well from a positive perspective. Take time to notice all the little wonderful things about your spouse, and dwell on these. It is amazing how differently we look at someone when we focus on positive traits.

7. Validate each other's feelings. Feelings are not right or wrong; they are simply feelings. And they are unique to the person experiencing them. No two people experience this empty-nest stage of marriage in exactly the same way. Talk about how you are feeling. Grief and loss are normal in this stage. Be patient with each other in your adjustments to this new phase; it will take time. Don't rush each other, but be willing to encourage and support each other.

8. Express appreciation to each other. Avoid taking each other for granted. Sharing words of affirmation and encouragement can make you both feel better about yourselves and about your marriage. The longer a couple has been together, the easier it is to take each other for granted. But sharing with your spouse how much you have appreciated him or her for all these years, and continuing to show that on a daily basis, will help your spouse feel treasured and loved. Consider writing your spouse a love note that expresses what he or she has meant to you for the many years you have been together, and then express how you want to spend the rest of your lives together.

9. Renew your commitment to spiritual growth. This is a perfect time to evaluate how you are doing on your spiritual growth. Although spiritual growth is a goal for most of us throughout our lives, we may not have paid as much attention to this during the parenting years as we would have liked. Now would be a great time to commit, both individually and as a couple, to begin growing again spiritually. Consider starting a Bible study together, join a small group, or pray together daily.

10. Get some rest. You may feel that you have been waiting your whole life for this, and maybe you have. You now have the time and the freedom to allow yourself to slow down the pace, relax, and catch up on years of needed rest. So enjoy! The time is yours! You have definitely earned it.

Saying "I Love You" All Over Again

As we conclude this section and this book, I want to remind you that your marriage is an investment that can yield a lifetime of returns. Always make the time to invest in your spouse and your marriage. As you do, you will find that God's blessing of a happy, healthy marriage is one of the best you could ever hope for.

No matter what stage of marriage you are in, make it a time of reconnection and renewal for the two of you. Take your spouse by the hands, look him or her in the eyes, and say ...

"I'd marry you all over again!"

TEN STEPS TO BUILDING YOUR SELF-ESTEEM

1. Learn to use positive self-talk. Positive self-talk is simply the act of saying positive things to yourself and focusing on your positive traits. It involves giving yourself compliments and affirming to yourself that you are a lovable, worthwhile, valuable person because God says you are. Just imagine saying this kind of statement to yourself every day and allowing yourself to believe it. I'm sure you would agree that you would begin to like yourself more.

2. Forgive yourself. In order to improve your self-esteem, stop living in the past and reliving your mistakes. Everyone makes mistakes. The difference between people with low self-esteem and those with healthy self-esteem is what they do with those mistakes. People with a healthy sense of personal identity are able to accept that they made a mistake and realize that it does not mean they are a failure. They can forgive themselves as God forgives them and then figure out what lesson they can learn from it and use it to make better choices in the future. My husband has always taught those around him that a mistake is a mistake only if you do not learn from it. If you do learn from it, then it is a learning experience (sometimes an expensive learning experience). It is only when we do not learn from what we did, either by choice or circumstances, that it really becomes a mistake.

3. Celebrate your strengths, successes, and talents. To build a healthy sense of self-esteem, learn to celebrate your successes, strengths, and talents. Make a list of small and large personal achievements, talents, and strengths. Allow yourself to really let it soak in as you consider this positive aspect of yourself. Remember, you didn't give yourself these talents, strengths, or opportunities. All things come to us through the hands of God our Creator.

4. Give of yourself and to yourself. The process of giving can lift your spirit faster than just about anything else. When you give *of yourself,* you focus on what you can do for others. As you give and contribute to those around you, you are useful and have something to offer to others. You feel more valuable—thus enhancing your self-esteem. When you give *to yourself,* you realize that you are a worthwhile, valuable, and lovable person and that you deserve to be given to. Avoid giving yourself just the leftovers. You deserve the best; indulge and pamper yourself often.

5. Accept compliments with a thank you. Your self-esteem will suffer as long as you do not allow others to give you compliments. When people downplay or even reject a compliment, it often because of low self-esteem. They do not believe good things about themselves, so they cannot believe the compliments. To improve your self-esteem, start right now accepting compliments with a smile and a thank you, and then really let them soak in. You deserve it!

6. Set realistic goals. Success builds self-esteem, and therefore we must learn to set ourselves up for success. If you set realistic goals and achieve them, you will like yourself better. Even small accomplishments and daily achievements can give you a boost. Start by evaluating your goals to determine if they are indeed realistic. Then break large goals down into smaller goals and eventually into daily or weekly goals that can be easily accomplished. Record your successes and completion of these smaller goals to keep yourself motivated and focused on the larger, long-term goals. Start with small goals and allow yourself to acknowledge these as successes once completed. Watch your confidence and self-esteem grow.

7. Stop comparing yourself to others. People with low self-esteem and a negative outlook on life often compare their lives to those who have more, accomplish more, earn more, and so forth. There will always be people out there who have more than you, no matter how much you have. Learn to live your own life; make your own decisions and reach for your own goals in order to strengthen your personal self-esteem. You were not created to accomplish what anyone else may accomplish. You were created to live your life and accomplish what God has asked you to do, and to do that to the very best of your ability. If you continue to struggle with a desire to compare yourself to others, try this on for a new perspective: Compare yourself only to those who have less than you, because they will always be out there also.

8. Try new things. People who struggle with low self-esteem also struggle with a lack of self-confidence. They do not believe in themselves or their abilities and therefore will avoid taking risks or trying new things. If you want to build your self-esteem, push yourself into new areas. Maybe you have always secretly wanted to play an instrument, participate in a sport, learn a foreign language, go back to school, jump out of an airplane, or take a hot-air balloon ride. Whatever it is, *try it!* Simply taking the risk, regardless of the outcome, can increase your self-confidence and desire to try again. Remember to avoid the negative self-talk and comparisons and just have fun.

9. Associate with encouragers, and become an encourager. First Thessalonians 5:11 says, "Therefore encourage one another and build each other up." And in Hebrews 3:13, we are told to "encourage one another daily." The types of people we associate with really do have an impact on how we feel about ourselves. If you surround yourself with negative people who are constantly putting you or themselves down, you begin to believe and agree with them. Consider how differently you will feel if surrounded by positive, supportive people who build you up, accept you as you are, and encourage you to grow. You will begin to think positively as well, and your self-esteem will grow.

10. Take control of your feelings. Often, people with low self-esteem, live their lives and make their decisions by how they feel at the moment. The problem with this is simple. Because of their low self-esteem they usually feel down; therefore, their decisions are going to be based on negative feelings. And a vicious and negative cycle begins that will only enhance the low opinion they already hold of themselves. They end up feeling controlled by their feelings, which can change at the drop of a hat. So to improve your self-esteem, you need to learn to act and think in positive ways, regardless of how you feel at the moment, and then trust that the feelings will begin to change—and they will.

HOW TO NOURISH A CONVERSATION

We can do several things to nourish and continue a conversation. Have you ever been in a conversation that seemed to die before it even got started? Or maybe you have tried to talk to a person whom you could just tell was not interested in what you had to say. On the other hand, have you ever walked away from talking to someone and thought, *Wow, I could have talked to her for hours and told her anything.* What's the difference? Most likely, that person's verbal and nonverbal communication made the difference. Let's look at some things that you can do to help your spouse feel he or she could talk to you for hours and tell you anything.

Keep Them Talking!

1. Use door openers. These are open, noncoercive invitations to talk. Often you can tell by the way a person is acting that she or he might want to talk but may be reluctant. If this person is your spouse, you want to draw him or her out gently. You want your spouse to talk, but you do not want to force a conversation. What do you do? You open the door and make yourself available by giving an invitation to talk. This can make it easier for the person to share whatever is on his or her mind because you took the first step by showing interest. Some examples of door openers are "Would you like to talk?"; "I'm here if you would like someone to talk to"; "I sense that something might be bothering you"; and, "I'd like to know what you think."

2. Demonstrate open and attentive body posture. The non-verbal communication of body posture can be powerful, and people pay attention to it whether we realize it or not. You communicate interest and attentiveness through your body by facing the person who is speaking, leaning slightly forward, and keeping your arms open. You can communicate nonacceptance and a lack of interest by turning your body away (even slightly), leaning back, or crossing your arms in front of your body.

3. Make good eye contact. Another important nonverbal communication is eye contact. Positioning yourself so that you can make good eye contact and then doing it shows interest and will likely help keep your spouse talking. The amount of eye contact should be comfortable and appropriate. If it is constant or intense, you may be communicating that you are disapproving, critical, or judgmental. However, if there is little or no eye contact, you may communicate lack of interest.

4. Use occasional encouragers. If you want something to happen, it usually helps to encourage it. If you want a conversation to continue and your spouse to keep sharing thoughts and feelings, then encourage him or her to do so without distracting from the communication. How do you do that? By sprinkling occasional encouragers throughout the conversation. These are brief indicators that let your spouse know you are interested and following the conversation. Some examples are "Tell me more"; "Yes"; "Really?"; "For instance?"; "Uh-huh"; and, "I see." Nodding your head is also an encourager.

5. Listen—really listen—by using ECHO conversation skills. Be sure to repeat to your spouse what you heard him or her say, especially the feelings your spouse seems to experience. To avoid interrupting, be careful to do this only after he or she has stopped talking.

6. Use open-ended questions. These questions are designed for the purpose of drawing out the person you are talking to. Used sparingly, they often will help the speaker sort out thoughts and feelings more thoroughly. Most people tend to use closed-ended questions that serve to cut a conversation short and often come across as if you know how the person feels or what the person should do. Closed-ended questions usually require only a one- or two-word answer. In contrast, open-ended questions tend to request further elaboration on the topic. Here are some examples of both open- and closed-ended questions:

Avoid these:	Instead say:
"Did that make you angry?"	"How did that make you feel?"
"Was it a horrible experience?"	"What was it like for you?"
"Don't you think you should tell your parents?"	"How do you think you should handle that situation?"

7. Focus on the relationship. In the process of a conversation, it is important to remember that the goal is to increase intimacy with your spouse. In other words, the conversation, the act of talking, the sharing of thoughts and feelings, causes the increased sense of connection between the two of you. However, we often can become distracted by the topic, and even more often by the solution. When this happens, we lose track of the importance of the connection we need. The most important part of a sharing time is not the solution but the feeling of intimacy. Level 4 and 5 conversations are not necessarily solution-based (see chapter 7). Although they may work toward a solution at times, it is more important that they include sharing for as long as necessary. Once a solution is presented, the conversation tends to be over. If your goal is to feel closer to your spouse, be careful to hold off on the solution until the sharing is complete.

READERS' GUIDE

FOR PERSONAL REFLECTION
OR GROUP DISCUSSION

INTRODUCTION

$\mathscr{S}$trong, healthy marriages do not just happen. And although keeping a marriage growing may not take a lot of hard work, it does require some daily attention. Failure to make the time and energy to give that daily attention is the biggest threat to marriages today. All couples, regardless of their stage of life, can find themselves quickly swallowed up by the countless activities and responsibilities this world has to offer. However, couples in the season of parenting are at the greatest risk of neglecting the marriage relationship.

If you hope to have a marriage that goes the distance and survives the parenting season, learn to focus on your marriage even while you are parenting. Although children require a lot of time and energy, they do not require *all* your time and energy. You cannot expect to put your spouse on hold for eighteen or more years and then just pick up where you left off. That's what this book has been about—learning how to remain partners while you are also parents.

As you begin this study, I encourage you to commit to sticking with it. This may be your first step to getting back on track and creating a couple-centered marriage. Children need parents who love each other and who stay together. So do it for your kids!

INTRODUCTION

The Game of the Century

1. What do you feel have been some of the major reasons for the breakdown of the "Parents team" over the past few decades?

2. Do you think the kids of today are really harder to parent, or are the parents of today being less effective? Why?

3. Where in your own family do you see your Parents team being less effective than it could be?

4. What are some of your children's best-developed strategies that have a negative impact on you as a couple?

5. How are kids affected when the parents do not work as a team? What do you think happens to the kids if the Parents team completely unravels and walks off the field?

6. How does a Parents team under God's management perform differently from one not under God's management?

Prayer Topic: Pray for families who are struggling to stay together. Ask God to make a difference in each family represented in your group. And pray that each couple will carve out the time needed to do this study.

CHAPTER 1

Where Did I Come From?

1. What did you learn from your parents about what marriage and parenting would be like? (You may want to review the list in this chapter.) Consider both the good and not-so-good aspects of what they

taught you. Which parts do you want to continue and what things would be better off replaced with something healthier?

2. "The more an individual understands his or her past, the greater the possibility that he or she will be able to control what he or she passes on to the next generation." Do you agree or disagree with this quotation? Why?

3. "Having a poor example in your parents is no excuse for being a poor spouse or parent yourself." Do you agree or disagree with this quotation? Why?

4. How much attention are you giving to your "rearview mirror"? Are you focused on your past, ignoring your past, or using your past to gain a sense of perspective? Explain. How much emphasis do you believe should be placed on your past?

5. What type of glasses do you tend to wear when looking at your past? Rose-colored, dark-colored, or clear? How do you think those glasses affect you?

6. When you consider your current relationship and parenting style, do you see yourself repeating patterns from your past? Maybe going to the opposite extreme? Or working to find a healthier middle ground? Explain.

7. Consider sharing with your spouse during this next week what you have learned about your past and how it is affecting you. Also consider asking your spouse to share with you how he or she may see patterns from your family of origin (good and bad) showing up in your current relationships.

Prayer Topic: Ask God to help you put your past in the proper perspective. Ask Him to reveal areas that need to be clearly looked at and resolved so as not to continue unhealthy patterns in your current family. Ask Him to help you forgive anything that may need to be forgiven.

CHAPTER 2

This Is Not What I Expected

1. Do you agree that your expectations have a major impact on your perceived marital satisfaction? Why or why not?

2. What are some of the ways your spouse's family different from yours? How are they similar? How have these differences and similarities affected your marriage and parenting?

3. Have you struggled with the concept that "different" does not mean "wrong"? How have you handled situations where you might have felt your way was the best or only or right way?

4. Make a list of the expections you hold for your spouse. ("I expect a good-bye kiss every morning"; "I expect dinner to be on the table by six o'clock.") As you review you list, mark each expectation that you and your spouse have never discussed. Will you drop the expectation or discuss it? When?

5. Consider sharing with the group about a time early in your marriage when your expectations were not met. How did the two of you work through that?

6. If you are experiencing unmet expectations within your relationship, do you believe it is because your spouse was never informed, your expectations are unrealistic, or your spouse is choosing not to meet your expectations? How might you go about resolving this?

Prayer Topic: Take time to thank God for the differences and the similarities you share with your spouse. Ask for patience and tolerance as you learn to accept each other's differences as well as for a willingness to let go of needing to have things your own way.

CHAPTER 3

How Much Do I Like *Me?*

1. "You cannot give what you do not possess." Do you agree or disagree with that statement? Why?

2. How do others know that you love yourself?

3. How did you feel when you did the "give God a grade" exercise in this chapter? If you are comfortable, share with the group whether or not the grade you gave God is the grade He deserved. If it was not, what will you do this week to align your grade with God's?

4. Are you showing that you value what God made through the way you care for yourself physically, emotionally, and spiritually? What can you do this week to nurture your body, mind, or spirit?

5. Luke 12:34 says, "Where your treasure is, there your heart will be also." Are your thoughts and actions showing that you are treasuring yourself? If not, what will you do to change your negative thoughts or actions?

6. Make a list of at least five things you like about yourself. Then make a list of at least five things you have done for yourself in the last two weeks. Share with the group at least one thing from each of these lists.

7. Review appendix A: "Ten Steps to Building Your Self-esteem." Of these steps, which do you struggle with the most? What one thing can you do this week to implement this step?

Prayer Topic: Take time to praise God and thank Him for what He created—you! Ask for His forgiveness if you have struggled with loving who you are or if you have not used your gifts or talents as He intended. Ask for His help as you learn to love yourself so you can better love others.

CHAPTER 4

How Do You Know That I Like You?

1. Share with the group an object or possession that you treasure. How would those around you know that you treasure it?

2. How did you and your spouse show the other that you treasured him or her while you were dating? Are you still doing those things today? Why or why not? Share with your spouse one or two things that he or she used to do that you would like him or her to start doing again.

3. Take a few minutes to review the components of TREASURE. Where do you see your personal strengths and weakness in showing the TREASURE-ing aspects to your spouse? What about your spouse? Where is he or she strongest and weakest in showing these to you?

4. Which of the TREASURE aspects is most important for you to receive from your spouse? Take a minute to share that with him or her.

5. On a daily basis, are you more focused on your spouse's positive or negative traits? Would your spouse agree with your answer? How does this affect your relationship?

6. The Golden Rule of marriage is "Do unto others as they need you to do." What will you do for your spouse this week that demonstrates this rule?

7. When was the last time you and your spouse went out on a date? If you haven't already done so, schedule your next one. For fresh ideas, ask other couples to share creative ways they have learned to date even while being parents.

Prayer Topic: Take time to really thank God for the treasure He provided for you in the form of your spouse. Ask for His guidance as you learn to show your spouse that you treasure him or her through your thoughts and actions.

CHAPTER 5

Time for a Time-out

1. How much time do the two of you spend together as a couple? Is this meeting each of your individual needs? If not, discuss ways to make more time for each other.

2. In asking each other the questions on page 81 this past week, what did you learn about each other?

3. Are you working harder at being a "superparent" or a "super-spouse"? How is this affecting your marriage?

4. What are some obstacles that keep you from spending time together as a couple? How will you overcome one of these obstacles this week?

5. What does it mean to "budget" your time? Are you budgeting your time? Are you putting the "big," important things in first? If not, how does this affect your time together as a couple?

6. Take time to write down the top five rungs on your "priority ladder." Now write what you think your spouse's top five are. Share these and compare how close they are. Look to see whether both you

and your spouse are in your top five. Are you surprised by what you see? Discuss.

7. Review the list of suggestions for "Creating Quality Time Together" at the end of the chapter. Which of these can you and your spouse commit to doing this next week?

Prayer Topic: Seek God's wisdom regarding the priorities in your life. Ask Him to reveal where your priorities currently fall and to help you in getting these back to where He intended them to be. Ask God to help you make time for each other.

CHAPTER 6

Can We Talk About It?

1. Do you feel you are a better listener or talker? Is your spouse a better listener or talker? How does that affect your relationship?

2. How do you think ECHO communication could help your marriage?

3. What did Dr. Cherry mean when she said that marriage is not "maintenance free"? Have you fallen into the trap of not attending to your marriage? How will you get out?

4. Identify and discuss the five levels of communication. At which level do you and your spouse spend most of your time? Why? Is your marriage suffering or growing based on the level of conversations you are having?

5. When was the last time you and your spouse had a serious and intimate conversation? How did this discussion affect your relationship?

6. Why do you think "touchdown" conversations are so difficult? Are you capable of "scoring a touchdown" (reaching level 5 conversation) when needed? If not, why not?

7. Review the information presented in appendix B: "How to Nourish a Conversation." Which of these skills do you and your spouse use in your conversations to keep each other talking?

Prayer Topic: Ask God to forgive you for the times you have been more interested in saying what you had to say than in taking time to listen to what your spouse needed to share. Commit to becoming a better listener.

CHAPTER 7

Avoid Getting Thrown Out of the Game

1. What do you think when you hear a couple say, "We never disagree or fight"?

2. Do you think it is realistic to expect that you and your spouse will never fight? Why or why not?

3. Does resolving a conflict mean that your spouse must eventually agree with you? Share a time when you and your spouse have had to "agree to disagree."

4. Do you agree that fighting can increase intimacy between you and your spouse? If so, how? Can there really be a win–win result in an argument?

5. How was anger and conflict handled in your home growing up? How has this affected how you handle anger and conflict now?

6. Review the four patterns of conflictual interactions presented in the chapter. Which, if any, of these do you see in your relationship?

7. What is a FAIR fight? Do you and your spouse fight FAIR? Do you believe beginning a conflict with a forgiving attitude would really make a difference? How?

8. Take time to make your own personal list of "Rules for FAIR Fighting" over the next week. Use the list of rules presented at the end of the chapter to get you started. Include those that are important for the two of you, and then add personal rules that may only apply to your relationship (i.e., no cussing, no finger pointing, stay in the room while talking, and so forth).

Prayer Topic: Ask for God's guidance as you and your spouse learn to handle anger and conflict in a healthy manner. Ask Him to help you to always have a forgiving attitude and a commitment to stick it out when things get tough.

CHAPTER 8

Whose Team Are You On?

1. How well do you feel you and your spouse are working together as a team? What are your strengths? What needs to improve?

2. Have you and your spouse developed a parenting "playbook" in which you have agreed on the various specific parenting interventions? If not, when will you?

3. Are you and your spouse presenting a united front to your children? If you are intentionally or unintentionally sabotaging each other. what can you do to change?

4. How do you handle it when you disagree with a parenting decision your spouse has made? If your response is ineffective, how will you change it?

5. When your children try the "mom-said-dad-said" tactic, how do you respond?

6. What strengths and weaknesses do each of you have as parents? How do you complement each other in these areas?

7. How do boundaries apply to marriage and parenting? Do you feel you and your spouse are setting healthy boundaries for yourselves and your children? Explain.

Prayer Topic: Thank God for putting the two of you together as a team, and for His being the "manager." Ask for His help as you work together to meet the challenges of parenting.

CHAPTER 9

Just Between You and Me

1. How have children affected your sexual relationship? Is one of you affected more than the other? Explain.

2. Have the two of you attempted to take shortcuts in this area of your relationship? If so, how have they worked out?

3. Describe some of the differences between men and women in regard to sex. What are your thoughts regarding the illustration that for men sex is like money and for women it is more like chocolate cake?

4. How do you feel about scheduling your sexual encounters? Why do you feel that way?

5. What is the difference between "making love" and "having sex"? Which do you consider to be the "most important" during the parenting season of your marriage?

6. Review the list of suggestions at the end of the chapter. Which of these suggestions do you feel might be most beneficial to your relationship at this point? How will you implement that suggestion?

Prayer Topic: Take time to thank God for the gift of sex. Ask Him to help you understand your differences and to focus on meeting each other's needs in this part of your relationship.

CHAPTER 10

And the Two Shall Become One

1. Did you adjust easily from dating to marriage? Or were these first few months or years really a workout for you? Explain.

2. Share a story of a time early in your marriage when you realized how different the two of you were from each other. How did you work it out?

3. What advice would you give a newlywed couple about how best to use these preseason training months or years? Or if you are a newlywed couple, what is the best advice you have received so far?

4. What are some of the different expectations the two of you held regarding children and parenting? (You may want to refer to the questions on page 156–157.)

5. Have you developed the habit of talking together every day? If not, how could you start carving that time out of your schedules? If you have, how has that time together benefited your relationship?

6. Evaluate whether your spiritual intimacy is growing. Share with each other how you would like to see this part of your relationship improve. How often do you pray together? How could you start doing this more?

7. Sometime this next week, make a list of things your spouse can do for you that make you feel loved. At the top of a sheet of paper write, "I feel loved when you ..." Then list as many specific things as you can think of that make you feel loved. Once you have both done this, exchange lists and start doing at least one thing from the list each week.

Prayer Topic: Thank God for your time together as a couple before having children. Ask Him to use this time to strengthen each of you and the bond between you. Commit to continuing to do for your spouse the things you have done during this early stage of marriage.

CHAPTER 11

When One Plus One Equals Three

1. What expectations did (or do) you have about the birth of your first child? What are some of the things you worried (or worry) about with regard to pregnancy, labor, and caring for an infant? Did you talk about these with your spouse? Why or why not?

2. What was (or is) the most difficult part of adjusting from couple to parents for each of you? How have you supported each other through these adjustments?

3. Do you think these early parenting adjustments are more difficult for husbands or wives? Why?

4. Of the two major threats to marriage during this stage (lack of time and lack of energy), which has affected you more? How can you and your spouse deal with this threat effectively?

5. How can the two of you maximize the limited time and energy you have available to you during this stage?

6. Is your marriage more couple centered or child centered? How does this affect your relationship?

Prayer Topic: Thank God for the miracle of a new baby. Thank Him for blessing your union with children. Ask for guidance and wisdom as you begin this parenting season and for help in keeping each other as a top priority.

CHAPTER 12

And They're Off!

1. If you consider your marriage to be like a garden that you prepared and planted during the dating stage, how does it look now? Have you continued to nourish and care for it? If not, what will you do this week to get it growing again?

2. Do you find it difficult to say no? Whom are you saying no to most often—spouse, kids, or the outside world?

3. Within your own household, are you overcommitted? Do you feel that every spare minute is filled with something? Where might you need to prune your schedule to allow more time just to be with your spouse?

4. How do you feel about making appointments to be with your spouse? If you have difficulty finding time to be together, will you schedule it?

5. Share some shortcuts you have learned to take that have helped you conserve time and energy.

6. How are you using family time to draw the two of you closer as a couple?

Prayer Topic: Take time to thank God for each of your children and their unique talents and gifts. Ask for help as you work together to manage this very hectic season of your life. Ask for God to reveal where you may need to adjust your schedule to allow the necessary family and couple time.

CHAPTER 13

Help! Get Me Out of Here!

1. Have you experienced conflicts between you and your teen that end up as conflicts between you and your spouse? Give an example. How will you avoid this in the future?

2. Have either of you felt that the other parent was sabotaging, or at least not supporting, your parenting decisions? How did you handle this?

3. What are the three main areas of conflict between teens and parents? Do you and your spouse agree on these areas? If not, how will you resolve the issues?

4. Do you agree with the concept that it is normal for a teen to push the limits and rebel? How have you noticed your teen pushing the limits? How have you responded as a parenting team?

5. How should parents respond to a destructive rebellion in their teen? How can you support each other in this process?

6. Do you believe you should keep secrets from each other if your teen asks you to? Does your spouse share your belief? If not, how will you resolve this issue?

7. How can you start preparing now for the next stage? How can you start the "letting go" of your teen? What is something the two of you can do together with the extra time that you are starting to have?

Prayer Topic: Take time to thank God for your teen. Ask God to unify you as parents in this challenging and difficult stage. Ask Him to reveal to you areas in which you are not working together as a team, and commit to making the necessary changes.

CHAPTER 14

You Don't Look Like the Person I Married!

1. Why do you think the divorce rate is on the rise in couples who have been married thirty or more years? Do you know of couples who made it this far and then divorced? Why do you think that was?

2. When the kids leave home, how might you and your spouse experience the feelings of loss and grief differently? How can you support each other?

3. How does your relationship need to be redefined at this stage? How do you think your marriage is going to look in the future? Have you shared new goals and dreams with each other?

4. What are some of the things you are looking forward to in this phase of your relationship? What are some of the things you are not looking forward to?

5. How do you expect your roles, responsibilities, and division of labor to change when the children are gone?

6. What kind of relationship are you hoping to have with your adult children? How do you plan to cultivate that desired relationship? How do you plan to deal with in-laws and grandchildren?

7. Write a love note this week to your spouse to say how much you have loved and appreciated him or her over the years.

Prayer Topic: Praise God for being with you through the parenting season. Recognize how He has helped and guided you. Thank Him for the blessing of your spouse and for this new season you are about to enter.

NOTES

Chapter 1
1. Dave Carder, et al. *Secrets of Your Family Tree: Healing for Adult Children of Dysfunctional Families* (Chicago, Ill.: Moody Press, 1991), 68.

Chapter 2
1. Chandler and Fittro, "Enhancing Midlife Marriage." http://www.ag.ohio-state.edu; Hamner and Turner, *Parenting in Contemporary Society,* 2nd Edition (New Jersey: Prentice Hall, 1990), 57; Jordon, Stanley, Markman, *Becoming Parents: How to Strengthen Your Marriage as Your Family Grows* (San Francisco: Jossey-Bass, 2001).

Chapter 4
1. Several studies as quoted in "Handling Marital Problems." *Psychological Self-help* (Mental Health Net), chap. 10, p. 2.
2. *New Webster's Dictionary of the English Language*; College Edition (New York: Consolidated Book Publishers, 1975), 1278.

Chapter 6
1. John Powell, *Why Am I Afraid to Tell You Who I Am?* (Allen, Tex.: Argus Communications, 1969). Adapted from pp. 54–62.

Chapter 7
1. Norman Wright, *Communication: Key to Your Marriage* (Ventura, Calif.: Regal Books, 1975), Introduction.
2. John Gottman, *Why Marriages Succeed or Fail: And How You Can Make Yours Last* (New York: Simon & Schuster Trade, 1999); Clifford Notarius and Howard Markman, *We Can Work It Out* (New York: Putnam, 1993).
3. Howard Markman, Scott Stanley, and Susan Blumberg, *Fighting for Your Marriage: Positive Steps for Preventing Divorce and Preserving a Lasting Love* (San Francisco: Jossey-Bass, 1996).
4. Ibid.
5. Debbie L. Cherry, *Discovering the Treasure of Marriage* (Colorado Springs, Colo.: Life Journey/Cook Communications, 2003).

Chapter 11
1. Guardian Unlimited, "The Truth about Babies," http://www.guardian.co.uk. Rick Hanson, Ph.D. and Jan Hanson, L.Ac., "Parents Are Negotiators," http://www.nurturemom.com. Nikki Cavalier Rabel, "When Baby Makes Three: Challenges of New Parenthood," Ohio State University, http://ohioline.osu.edu. Nicole Martin, "Deciding to Have Children Special Report," http://www.handpen.com.
2. Mary Longo, "The Impact of Infants on Family Life," Ohio State University, http://ohioline.osu.edu.

Chapter 14
1. David Arp and Claudia Arp, *The Second Half of Marriage* (Grand Rapids, Mich.: Zondervan, 1998); David Arp, Claudia Arp, Scott Stanley, Howard Markman and Susan Blumberg, *Empty Nesting: Reinventing Your Relationship When the Kids Leave Home* (San Francisco: Jossey-Bass, 2001).
2. Debbie L. Cherry, *Discovering the Treasure of Marriage* (Colorado Springs, Colo.: Life Journey/Cook Communications, 2003).

The Word at Work Around the World

A vital part of Cook Communications Ministries is our international outreach, Cook Communications Ministries International (CCMI). Your purchase of this book, and of other books and Christian-growth products from Cook, enables CCMI to provide Bibles and Christian literature to people in more than 150 languages in 65 countries.

Cook Communications Ministries is a not-for-profit, self-supporting organization. Revenues from sales of our books, Bible curricula, and other church and home products not only fund our U.S. ministry, but also fund our CCMI ministry around the world. One hundred percent of donations to CCMI go to our international literature programs.

CCMI reaches out internationally in three ways:

- Our premier International Christian Publishing Institute (ICPI) trains leaders from nationally led publishing houses around the world.

- We provide literature for pastors, evangelists, and Christian workers in their national language.

- We reach people at risk—refugees, AIDS victims, street children, and famine victims—with God's Word.

Word Power, God's Power

Faith Kidz, RiverOak, Honor, Life Journey, Victor, NexGen — every time you purchase a book produced by Cook Communications Ministries, you not only meet a vital personal need in your life or in the life of someone you love, but you're also a part of ministering to José in Colombia, Humberto in Chile, Gousa in India, or Lidiane in Brazil. You help make it possible for a pastor in China, a child in Peru, or a mother in West Africa to enjoy a life-changing book. And because you helped, children and adults around the world are learning God's Word and walking in his ways.

Thank you for your partnership in helping to disciple the world. May God bless you with the power of his Word in your life.

For more information about our international ministries, visit www.ccmi.org.

Additional copies of *CHILDPROOFING YOUR MARRIAGE*
and with other Life Journey titles
are available from your local Christian bookseller.

If you have enjoyed this book,
or if it has had an impact on your life,
we would like to hear from you.

Please contact us at:

LIFE JOURNEY BOOKS
Cook Communications Ministries, Dept. 201
4050 Lee Vance View
Colorado Springs, CO 80918
Or visit our Web site: www.cookministries.com